PUT YOUR HANDS UP
(An Arrest Warrant From God)

POLICE

Robert D. Faubel
Retired Police Officer

Foreword by Pastor Al Stewart

Revised

PoBoy Publishing © 2023

REVISED 2023 EDITION

Table of Contents

Foreword

I was excited when my friend of over 30 years and former video editor of my TV program, who is a retired Police Officer and Chaplain, told me he was ready to write this book. It is a basic biographical insight into his life as well as the rigors and obstacles those who place themselves in harm's way on our behalf go through. We are all deeply appreciative of what they do on a daily basis.

Friends, my prayer is that as you read through the powerful pages of this book, like Bob, you too can go from a place of trusting only in yourself to where Bob eventually traveled in his life, a place of strong faith in our living Lord Jesus Christ. Notice how God uses what we can only see as tragedy, how He speaks in that *"still small voice"* through various circumstances. We need only to be listening to that voice!

The Bible tells us in Deuteronomy 29:29 that *"the secret things belong to the Lord"*. Reading through Bob's manuscript time and time again I saw many *"secret"* things taking place throughout his life. God used all of them and I have NO doubt He will use yours as well as you read.

"Put Your Hand's Up!" Is a well written, refreshingly raw and honest account of how the Lord eventually brought Bob to Himself and of how He desires to do the same to the readers of this book.

Rev. Al Stewart, D.D.

Rev. Al Stewart, D.D.
Senior Pastor,
Great Grace Chapel of Daytona Beach

Dedication To Law Enforcement

This was written as a testimony to Police Officers and to all about how God changes lives. It is therefore dedicated to all Law Enforcement for their personal dedication to this occupation which is found in the Bible.

Police Officers deal with physical and mental reality 24/7, on the job and off. We are the "frontline" between the civil population and the evil attempting to destroy it. Behind this reality is the spiritual reality which can only be understood by those seeking it.

This book is inspired by my Lord Jesus Christ. He is the one who gives me the wisdom every day through his Holy Spirit. There are no words that can express my love for Him in the things he has done for me all my life. I have gone from believing only in what touches my senses to believing in something that doesn't touch my senses and is beyond anyone's imagination.

What I have written shows how I went from point "A" to point "B". I show what my life was like as a child growing up in my home where there was no mention of God, Jesus Christ, or the Bible except in negative applications. My intention is to show how I was influenced in this type of home life leading me to that which I believed in.

I want to thank my wife and all the people who have inspired me to give my testimony with the intention of changing lives, to open the eyes of the blind so that they may see the truth.

It has been quoted, *"Walk a mile in my shoes"*. Put on a badge and a weapon, go out into the world and people's lives, and you will know what it is like to be a Police Officer. Officers are on the front lines 24/7 for you and me. Lately, officers are being killed in the line of duty like no other time because of the changes in our society. The Bible predicted that before Jesus Christ returns, the world would be in much chaos like has never been seen before.

The Bible is either right or it is wrong. Is there a God or isn't there a God? The problem is that once you die there is no "undo" button. There is no forgiveness after death. NOW is the time for you to seek the truth as I did and thousands of other law enforcement officers around the world have done.

And so it is . . .

 Introduction

I wrote this book about the events and situations that occurred in my life leading up to the time that I gave my life to Jesus Christ. These situations happened in the New York and Connecticut areas of the United States of America.

You might be from a different part of the USA or even a different part of the world and therefore, you might not be able to relate to my life situations especially the TV shows that I watched and games that I played but that is not the point of this book.

Don't look at the trees but look at the forest. The concept in this book is about how I grew up in an environment where God was not brought up until one day when someone approached me.

We all are a product of our environment. We have the choice, as adults, of allowing certain things and people into our lives. When we are children under our parents, we can't always control what happens to us. This book is about that environment and how I was conditioned into believing that God did not exist until I was challenged.

The goal of this book is to challenge the reader into looking at his/her life and what you allow in your life. I am challenging YOU to seek God for your life and to allow Jesus Christ to be your Lord and Savior.

Revelation 12:11

They conquered him

by the blood of the Lamb

and *by the word of their testimony*,

for they did not love their lives

in the face of death.

Chapter One

My TV Show Life!

Dispatcher: *"H.Q. to 406."*

Me: *"406, go ahead."*

Dispatcher: *"25C, Lake and Segar Signal 3 en route. 17 en route."*

Me: *"25C, 10-4. En route, responding Code 1. Send the hook."*

That discourse I would hear many times within my employment as a police officer, of almost 25 years. Responding to those types of emergencies can be life threatening for officers as well as the general public. But there was always something inside of me that never allowed me to fear in those circumstances. That *"something"* I would learn later in years to come.

I am a *"Baby-Boomer"* born in 1950 with no brothers or sisters. When I was born, my parents were living in Wyandanch, Long Island, New York and when I was 4 years old, we moved to Massapequa, a middle-class suburbia. I can still picture driving up in the driveway to our new home. It was a 2 bedroom, Cape Cod type home with a separate garage. This garage was rarely used for the cars. It was more of a playhouse, fort and a treasure chest of many items. A great *"Hide and Seek"* place!

To give you an idea of the era I grew up in and what life was like in my family, it is necessary to explain a few things showing how my life progressed from God being void to a place where I finally acknowledged Him. The sun is always out but is hidden when clouds appear. God is always there, but He is silent many times for a reason.

The 1950's was a time where people didn't lock their doors at night and neighbors got together on a regular basis. Children could ride their bikes for blocks in safety. My generation invented the skateboard by cutting up a wooden board, taking apart our metal roller skates and attaching them to each end of the board. I also learned through many attempts what the term *"balance"* means from riding that skateboard! Mom also had plenty of *"Band-Aids"*.

We played *"Tag"* and used chalk to make the bases in the road for baseball. Every boy had his shoe box full of baseball cards and a separate box for the extra cards he could trade with. Mickey Mantle, Roger Maris and Willie Mays were the top cards to trade. I would be quite wealthy right now if I had kept all those cards! Can you imagine! Do kids today know what baseball cards are?

The cards we didn't care for were clipped to the spokes of our bikes with wooden clothes pins we took from our moms clotheslines, to make the bikes sound like motorcycles. Stores were closed on Sundays while people went to church. Can you imagine stores today being closed on Sunday? When the *"Good Humor"* man*(ice cream truck)* came around, you could hear all the kids screaming, *"Mom, the Good Humor man is here!"* and the race to get to his truck first for that Toasted Almond or Strawberry Shortcake ice cream on a stick. *"Mister Softee"* was also popular then.

Life was like the TV shows, *"Leave It to Beaver, Lassie, Zorro, Roy Rogers, Mr. Rogers, Davy Crockett, the Mickey Mouse Club, Sky King, My Friend Flicka, Kukla, Fran and Ollie"* and others. These were shows that parents didn't have to worry about the content. Men didn't wear tights and women didn't show any cleavage! Can you imagine?

All the shows were clean and had good morals with the bad guy losing all the time. The bad guys wore black and the good guys wore white! There was no gender question or overt discrimination. Believe it or not, there was no swearing on TV! Imagine that! Many channels would actually sign off at midnight with only their color bars seen. In the morning the channels would turn back on and play the national anthem!

Discipline was real! If you got into trouble, your mother spanked you and in some cases took a switch to you. Today, they would be arrested for assault. Teachers in school could grab you by the collar and walk you down to the principal's office where your parents were called at work! They were not too happy about that! You were also taught to never call adults by their first name. Today, schools would probably call in a swat team if some kid got spanked and the news people would arrive with their cameras to make sure it got on social media! Facebook and Twitter would light up!

Respect for adults was taught all the time because they represented authority and as you grew up, that respect was supposed to apply to all types of authority, especially police officers. Not today! We learned respect for authority in those days or got a good spanking! Yes, spanking was the *"norm"* then. The phrase that was heard in many homes was, *"Wait 'til your father gets home!"* Today in some homes it might be, *"Wait 'til your mother gets home"* or you might be *"blocked"* on Facebook!

You obeyed the teacher or she would have you sit in the corner. I was never really a bad boy in grade school. I still have all my grade school class pictures. Putting a tie on for those pictures was a big deal and made me proud to wear one. After lunch though, I would take it off and stuff it in my Roy Rogers metal lunch box next to my thermos and Twinkies. This was OK with Mom except the times when I didn't finish my peanut butter and jelly sandwich. The tie didn't fare well. I tried licking off the jelly but my Mom could tell and she would say, *"You forgot to lick the peanut butter off also!"*

Good character is developed over a period of time. I could see how God was arranging things in my life for the future. Kids in this era had to use creativity in order to have fun. Creativity can develop character. We didn't have all the electronic gadgets that are available now. We had Frisbees, Hula Hoops, cap guns, army men, hand puppets, Lincoln Logs and Erector sets. We used chalk on the sidewalk for Hopscotch and broom handles for stick ball.

During the summer, water pistols were a craze along with water balloon fights. Did you ever have "chicken fights"? Playing tag was a favorite which usually ended in a small argument if you got "tagged". Someone usually got hurt from playing kickball because the ball hit them in the face. Of course, then there was "Dodge ball" where getting hit was the point of the game. There were times that I got hit with a ball or tripped running to bases but we did our best not to cry in front of our friends. Then there was the time that I was running to a base, tripped and fell right into a pile of dog poop! Yes, I could hear the laughter from the other kids but got up and chased them with it! Poop was all over!

We used to get our father's handkerchiefs, and tie string and metal nuts to each of the four corners of the handkerchiefs. Then we would throw them as high up into the air as possible and watch them slowly come down like a parachute. That was creative! The problem was that sometimes they landed on the wires on the telephone poles. My Dad was not too happy that I was always using his handkerchiefs to give to the other guys.

What did you do as a kid to play with other kids? I had no influence to learn some basic concepts in life. It's kind of odd that much of my influences came from TV and yet today much influence for kids comes through the social media which is another form of TV! The cell phone has replaced the TV in many ways.

When I came home from grade school I would turn the black and white TV on *(can you imagine no color TV!)* to watch Officer Joe Bolton and Superman! I was always so thrilled to see Officer Joe. My hero! One of my favorite games was *"Cops and Robbers"* and I was always the cop. I had gotten a gold plated toy gun and holster and I thought I was hot stuff! The policeman was always the *"Good Guy" (and of course Firemen were on the hero list also!)*

In that era, there were no religious type shows like there are today. I never saw my parents watching anything remotely religious though I do recall Oral Roberts coming on TV once in a while.

Each day in grade school, we would say the Pledge of Allegiance to the flag and sometimes the teacher would have us all pray for a classmate who was sick. Today kids get expelled from school because they prayed or had some religious shirt on! When I was growing up, there were no public atheists except well know musicians.

My life began with influence from the materialistic things of life. God knows that we live in a materialistic world and it would be many years later that I would learn how this world effects us in good and bad ways. We are all bombarded by the material world and it's influences but God gave us the ability to make choices in life. Search your life and see what you allow to influence you. It's always easy to make excuses for what we do each day. What you watch and who you hang around will change you. That's who we are as human beings. Is God any part of your life? What about your kid's lives?

Chapter Two

Home Sweet Home

God was not a real factor in my life living in Massapequa. My father was a German atheist and my mother was an Irish Catholic. How that combination was created, I never knew. My father never went to church. He always said the Bible was just a story and that it was not true. Somehow though, they must have come into some type of an agreement and I found myself going to an Episcopal Church right in back of the Catholic Church.

I remember going to Sunday school where I got my first Bible and I still have it! The best part about going there was the last Sunday of each month we were allowed to attend the service upstairs. I looked forward to it each month. There was just something that appealed to me about being in that service. Of course, as a child, I couldn't explain it. My parents never sat me down to talk about God at all. The only initial experience about the Bible came from that Sunday school. My friends in the neighborhood never mentioned God either but they did go to church.

My father was a used car salesman and my mother worked a comptometer which basically was the original calculator. She worked for Republic Aviation. He worked six days a week and my mother worked five.

Sundays, my father worked his crosswords puzzles and watched the games on TV. My mother was in the kitchen cooking and preparing meals while I played with my green army men and my cap gun. I had my cars and trucks and other assorted toys. This was normal for boys.

There was always something to do and you had to use your imagination to create your fun. I didn't own a tent so I took blankets and hung them off the back of the couch connected to 2 chairs in front of the couch. They were my inside forts!

I was also taught to do *"chores"* like mowing the lawn, raking leaves, cleaning windows, making my bed, mopping the floors. Do kids learn these things today? It's hard to do that stuff with a cell phone in your hand!

My mother was strict and alcohol didn't help the matter at all. One day when I was 11 years old, I came home from school and was playing with our dog. Fooling around, he bumped into a bookcase knocking over my mother's crystal candelabra smashing it into pieces! To say the least, my mother was not a happy camper! When she got home, I didn't say a thing. What was I thinking that she wouldn't notice?

After dinner when she sat down with a couple of "high balls", she finally noticed the candelabra missing and she went off the wall! I told her what had happened and she had me strip my clothes off. She began to beat me with an extension cord on my back for about 10 minutes. Just then my father came home and stopped her, took me aside and dealt with the "marks" on my back. Then the shouting began and dishes flew. God was not too visible in this situation at all though I did hear His name expressed a couple of times.

It's pretty vague now but there were other times that were similar. She used to keep a "cat o' nine tails" in the kitchen drawer and only hit me twice with it, very sad. Today, she would have been arrested.

My parents were never the type to play with me or do much of anything with me. I never really had that "*connection*" with them. I basically kept alone. But not all life was bad. Don't get the idea that I lived in a concentration camp. We did go to amusement parks, 1964 World's Fair, different beaches, big family get together's, and such but we never went to church together. The world went to church on Sunday but my parents did not. They were not members of that persuasion.

Both my parents were alcoholics and smoked at least 2 packs of cigarettes a day. When I was 15, I stole a pack of my father's "*Kool*" cigarettes from his closet and went over to my friend's house. He had a fort in the backyard. This is where I lit up my first cigarette, turned green, dry heaved and never smoked again! I can still picture that fort! God probably had something to do with that! Cigarettes won't send you to hell but it will make you smell like you've been there and back!

"*High Balls*" as I mentioned were my parent's drink of choice at home. They had a drink every night. We rarely ever went out but they had a number of parties at home or over the neighbor's homes. I loved the parties because I could spend the night over at my buddy's house. He had bunk beds and a built in pool! His father was a volunteer fireman so it was impressive when he parked a fire truck in front of his house!

Growing up, I always wanted to be the hero. I was always the cop in "*cops and robbers*" and the sheriff playing "*cowboys and Indians*". I watched all the hero TV shows and was overjoyed when I got my first cowboy gun and holster! It was "*Mattel's Fanner Fifty*" which could shoot caps! I slept with that gun and had gotten a Roy Rogers shirt and cowboy hat. I thought I was the star of the block until I saw one of my friends with the same outfit.

I was 12 years old on March 17th, 1962, when my father took us out for a St. Patrick's Day dinner at a special restaurant next to a movie theatre. Afterwards we planned go to see the movie, *"Wonderama, The 7 Wonders of the World"*. This was a big deal as my mother being Irish. I was excited because we rarely ever did this. When we arrived at this fancy restaurant, we were escorted to a table.

After about 10 minutes, my father said, *"Alice, I don't feel so good. I'm going to the bathroom."* He got up, walked about 10 feet, collapsed with a massive heart attack! I remember riding in the front seat of the Cadillac ambulance.

I could hear my father screaming in the back, *"Somebody help me! God please help me!"* He would repeat that all the way to the hospital. I don't remember much more except being in a room with my mother when a priest came in and said that my father had passed away. I hated that priest! I wasn't too happy with God either. So, where was God? I thought, my father didn't believe in God but called out his name when he had the heart attack. I never went back to church again. Strangely, 20 years later I would be on my knees at an altar asking God to run my life!

The whole situation is vague now maybe because I suppressed all the hurt. The next day I remember wearing my sports jacket going to the funeral parlor where all our relatives and neighbors were gathered. We drove to the Long Island cemetery where he was buried as a veteran of WW 1. Yes, *WW 1*.

He was born in 1900 and lied about his age to get into the Army. He was a 2nd LT when he got out. My mother would eventually be buried there also. Afterwards, we had the usual *"after the funeral"* get together at home. I wonder where God was in my parents lives. How many times did God make himself aware to them but they just did not see Him. We all have questions for God. Do you ever ask God, where are you? Do you ask Him, why God? Why did this have to happen to me?

Growing up, I rarely ever saw a police officer except in certain places like going to Jones Beach. This place was very popular and many people went there because it was the *"cool"* place to be. It was there, I guess, that I got my real first up close look at a police officer when I was 10.

This beach had a big boardwalk and officers regularly patrolled it. I had seen a number of kids get into fights and officers would respond. Standing there, watching them handcuff violators and deal with the crowd, gave me a great impression of police officers. They were the ones *"in charge"* and dealt with the situation. It left an impression on me.

Everyone admired the police officer. They were the *"heroes"*. All the TV shows where police were involved showed them respectfully. Between watching the cop shows and seeing officers first hand, probably started my unconscious desire to wear that uniform. I always loved playing the good guy! Was this God preparing me for the future?

Proverbs 16:9

A man's heart plans his way,

but the Lord determines his steps.

Chapter Three

On the Road Again

In summer of 1962, my mother lost her job for reasons I never knew, but I have suspicions now because of her alcoholism. With no income, she was forced to sell the house and we moved to Danbury, Connecticut because one of our former neighbors had moved there. Of course, those neighbors became present friends again.

I was 12 at the time and finished 8th grade in Danbury. My mother never talked about God and we never went to church. We followed the traditional Christian holidays like Easter and Christmas but that was about it. Like many other people, Easter was about the Easter bunny and eggs and Christmas was about Santa. No one mentioned Jesus or the Bible.

As I recall, St. Patrick's Day was never the same any more. Mom would make the traditional corned beef, cabbage and potatoes. She had stopped decorating with Irish carnations as she used to do. She only did things out of conditioned tradition.

She was becoming depressed because she was alone and there was no family to help support her. The drinking increased which I could understand now that I'm older. She even tried attending a group called, *"Parents without Partners"* but eventually that faded away. I ask, why didn't she go to a church?

In 1964, I remember sitting on the floor of our friend's house with my mother and his mother sitting behind us, watching the Beatles on the Ed Sullivan show for the first time. I was 14 and now I wanted to play guitar in a band so bad! Like other boys, after seeing the Beatles, we felt we were meant for stardom!

During these years, God or church was not part of the picture at all. I was slowly being conditioned into thinking, *"seeing is believing!"*

In high school everyone talked Beatles this and Beatles that. We all knew the lyrics to all the latest songs from them. There was the time when John Lennon said they were more popular than Jesus!

1964 through 1968 were my high school years where you learn a lot more than academics and not about God. I got my first guitar and my friend Pat got some cookies sheets for drums and we started a band. A short time later I met Alan who got his guitar and we were a trio! As time went on, we got real equipment and played at dances, *"band competitions"* and *"stag night"* at the Elks Club on Friday nights.

The 60's revolution was upon us and we had a great time and made many memories. I don't recall anything pertaining to God during these years. Without a father and no real influence from my mother other than reprimands, I learned about life from what I encountered.

There was no God in the world around me. We lived in a world where fun was derived from physical things like ice cream, TV, toys, games and good friends. You didn't learn to look at yourself with honesty. Self-gratification was in things. Spirituality was not a part of my life.

You can see that all these situations were creating a mindset that was far from God. I have asked God why He didn't send a Christian my way when I was young.

At 16, I did something stupid. I was driving around throwing firecrackers out my window while I was actually driving! *(I know, you don't have to say it! It was stupid!)* Sure enough, I saw the red rotating lights behind me. He was very nice but chewed me out and took the rest of the fire crackers. He let me go! Now that might have been an encounter with God getting me out of that situation but it was my first personal encounter with a police officer. God is merciful!

In high school I had some good friends. We had our party times. Good times were had at the drive-in theater! We all had our fun times but the things we were involved in were clean fun. Drugs were just not prevalent with us. Even the kids I hung with, I don't remember them smoking. I also don't remember them talking about God at any time. The only time I remember hearing God was on television shows of that time like *"Ozzie and Harriet"* or perhaps something like *"Lassie"*.

But not all the memories during high school were great. When we had moved to Danbury, we moved into a mobile home park. This was a big change from moving from a house into a mobile home.

My mother was drinking more heavily than before. It was very sad and I was depressed. There was one night when she was sleep walking and woke me up. She didn't appear to be sleeping at all! She called her boss at 2 am and didn't realize she did so. Then she had me iron bed sheets. I muttered something about doing that and she came over and punched me in the jaw! I couldn't believe she did that! Life was not good then.

Even though she had her days, she always kept a clean home. Dishes were always done and beds made each day. She did teach me discipline and to never lie. She cooked and took care of me but life with an alcoholic was extremely hard. There were times after school when I didn't want to come home. After I graduated from high school, I joined the US NAVY.

Isaiah 40:31

but those who trust in the Lord

will renew their strength;

they will soar on wings like eagles;

they will run and not grow weary;

they will walk and not faint.

Chapter Four

Anchors Away

1968 was one of the most memorable years in American history as well as mine. Many famous events occurred such as the assassination of Martin Luther King; Robert Kennedy was mortally wounded when he was shot by Sirhan Sirhan.

The peace movement had continued to grow and more Americans were against the war in Vietnam. There was a Flu Pandemic in Hong Kong and the first Black power salute was seen on Television worldwide during an Olympics medal ceremony. You can look up all the events that went on that year but the biggest for me was joining the US NAVY.

In the military, you wake up to another reality. It's raw and it's hard. They don't care about your emotions and they will do everything to break you. To say the least, there was no God in boot camp!

It's the place where you learn what the term *"respect"* means especially to authority. Weakness was not permitted or you were out! To give you an example, we all took turns doing the *"Dipsy Dumpster"* watch. You had to stand guard for 8 hours *"guarding"* a dumpster and I was there during the winter!

We had to go to the gym, get on our knees and elbows, holding our rifles. Then we had to crawl on our knees and elbows to the end of the gym! It's called *"breaking"* you. The NAVY is where I learned how people used God's name in a different manner.

In retrospect, my life was being conditioned into thinking reality is what was physically before me. If not, it didn't exist. This is the way the world was and still is today. We all have to deal with the physical reality of life. Yet, we don't take time to think about how the physical began.

The winter of 1968 was cold at the Great Lakes Training center. When you first arrive, they herd you into a big gym where you stand in painted blocks on the floor and strip off your clothes to your underwear. You walk over to another room and they hand you denim uniforms. Then it's off to the barber where you lose all your hair! What a sight that was!

After that it's off to where they push you in a deep pool to see if you can swim! When you're in the NAVY, they find out right away if you can swim. It works every time! Ships don't work on Ground! God was not a part of my life there, even though we went to services in the big hall. That is when I heard the NAVY choir. When they sang, I actually got choked up! They were incredible!

After boot camp, I was sent to Quartermaster School in Newport, Rhode Island where I learned how to navigate a ship. It was the first time I witnessed a girl being raped by multiple assailants. When parents don't teach you about sex before getting into the world, you learn by experience. The problem is learning can be done in the wrong manner and obtaining an unreal concept. Sex was meant to be beautiful with your wife.

Upon graduating from that school, I was assigned to the USS Guadalcanal in Norfolk, Virginia. This ship was a helicopter carrier. When we were on tours, we carried 1500 marines. It's similar to the big carriers but smaller. I toured the whole Caribbean, England and Denmark. At 19 years old, I was steering an aircraft carrier! What an experience that was! Basically I was a taxi driver for Marines!

For the next 2½ years I would experience new things that would shape my belief system. I saw riches and famines. I saw diseased people and sexual exploitation. There was a guy on board who tried to tell me about Jesus and I just didn't want to hear it. All the bad things I experienced in the NAVY and thinking about my parents, I wondered if there was a God. Where was He? I had met a couple of guys who said they were Christians but never acted like what I thought a Christian should act like. I actually thought I was a Christian because I wasn't Jewish! I thought people were either one or the other. When you're in the military, God is not seen except by a few going to church.

Learning about firearms was a part of my training and the first time I shot a .45, I thought I would need a new arm. The older guys just laughed but I eventually was able to fire it properly. M-16's were a part of the training also since the Vietnam war was in full swing. The next time that I would wear a side arm, I would be wearing a badge also. It would also be a time when I would point it at someone ready to shoot to kill!

You have to understand that I left the home of an alcoholic at 18 and went straight into the service. I did not grow up in a Godly home. I was not a drinker. Even if I had wanted to drink, my mother would have slammed me.

So here I am a young *"buck"* in the service that never did any real drinking. When we were in port in Norfolk, the routine in our division was cleaning and polishing the brass and making sure all the clocks on the ship were wound. 56 clocks had to be wound! There were other things we did but at 1600 hours, the work day was done! We went to Burger King, 7-Eleven and parked somewhere to eat.

Now picture this: I am in the passenger seat and 3 guys in the back. One of the guys in the back opens a new bottle of Johnny Walker and starts to hand it around for everyone to get a slug. Then they hand the bottle to me, the *"kid".* I said no, but they prodded me to drink. So I drank . . . . half the bottle! Just had to do that so called *"manly"* thing! The only thing I can remember is being carried up into the ship and being placed in my bottom bunk. Then I rolled over and puked my brains out! I am sure none of you went through this!

Yes, growing up in the military had its moments. Some I'm sure I have forgotten. Some I can remember clearly such as being in port of San Juan for a month at a time. I would be getting a deep tan and singing by the pool of a hotel getting free Piña Coladas!

My tan was so dark that hotel visitors sometimes thought I was a native! I also remember my Chief petty officer canceling my weekend leave because I didn't buff the pilot house floor to his liking! I see now that he must have been a demon!

There were many good and bad times in the NAVY, I believe that helped me in developing who I was going to become. There was one influence that never entered my life at that time . . . God. Looking back of course, I know now that God was guiding my steps.

It's very easy to live your life by what you see. I grew up that you don't talk about politics and religion. While I was away in the NAVY, my mother was at home doing very poorly, medically and emotionally. Her drinking was taking its toll. She began to write letters to congressmen and clergy to get me released from the NAVY. At the time, I was happy to leave but embarrassed that I had an alcoholic mother.

One day on the ship, I get called into the ship's office where an officer handed me a paper and told me that I was being released from the NAVY with an Honorable Discharge! There were no words that I could express but overwhelming joy! Maybe God was working in my life? The guys who had a couple of years left were not too happy that I was getting out ahead of them!

Chapter Five

I'm a Free Man

Arriving back in Connecticut, I lived with my mother because I had no other place to go. It didn't take but a month to understand that in no way that this 21 year old *"NAVY man"* was going to live with his mother who was instituting rules for living at home and what time I was allowed to stay out until. You see, I was now a *"man of the world"*, I was a free man! My mother wasn't about to tell me how to live! She suggested to me about going to a church but that was not about to happen. She would talk about God once in a while but very seldom.

Having seen what I saw in the NAVY, God was not real to me. God was a name in a book. I couldn't see God, so he didn't exist. But I would learn later that just because you can't see it, doesn't mean it's non existent. Can you see, feel, hear or taste air? You see the result if it's actions.

Life at home though, was getting bad because of her drinking. I decided that maybe it was time to go to college and since there was a college right there in Danbury, I would apply. Being a veteran, I applied for VA benefits which helped me through my college career.

In September of 1971 I became a freshman in college. I met new people who convinced me to run for Vice President of the class. This started my social life which opened doors to a new world. After all, my whole life had been controlled by someone or some organization. I was not used to the freedom that was upon me instantly. It was like any form of authority went out the window and I was in charge!

There was no God on campus *(aside from religious groups)* and the only time I heard His name used was in some profanity. I'm sure that if you have been on a campus, you know what I am talking about. The only religion was partying which is unfortunate. Today though, more Christian groups are forming despite the growing liberalism on college campuses.

My first encounter with law enforcement at this time was with campus security and Danbury Police when they had to break up fights in the dorms. You have to understand that cops were not desired on campus since they represented the *"establishment"*. This mindset was the prevailing thought during that time and probably still is today. Campus security officers were just *"one of the gang"* and really didn't enforce anything unless it was obvious and the administration forced the issue.

I got very involved with the social life on campus including being a member of many organizations. I went to classes for the most part but dropped some courses due to lack of interest. Most of the courses I enjoyed and got a lot out of them for the future. My major was Psychology because I loved people and wanted to deal with them. My goal was to be a Clinical Psychologist. But there were underlying reasons why I needed to be involved with so many organizations.

I understand now that I have the Biblical gift of serving along with a few other gifts. Growing up, I was involved with different groups like Cub Scouts, Boy Scouts and Explorers. I also had joined the Allied Nautical Cadets. It's strange now when I think about it how the Boy Scouts always promoted *"God and Country"* yet never spoke about God or the Bible and my Troop and Post were both in a church! You never heard any of  the Scout leaders talk about God. Today they are even taking the word *"Boy"* of of the name *"Boy Scouts"*!

There were many groups to get involved with on campus. I was class vice-president my Freshman year but was president the next 3 years. Since social life was abundant I became the Fall, Winter, and Spring chairman organizing all the events. This experience allowed me to meet famous rock groups like Jay and the Americans, the Turtles, Sha Na Na, the Four Seasons, and many other groups and individuals.

The Bible talks about how the cares and events in our lives lure us away from what God has intended for our lives. It's not that God doesn't want us to be involved or to have nice things, it's just that He wants us to allow Him to run our lives and to show us what corrupts our lives. He doesn't want the world's way of thinking to run our lives. As you can see today, much of the world's concepts are anti-God.

This is a problem with many families because proper upbringing is just not done. If kids are not given the right training, they will inherently seek out what they need. Therefore, many kids grow up with the wrong morals or beliefs. They become a product of their environment and live according to that environment. I was never taught about feeling convicted of something I did wrong. Even though I was reprimanded for things that I did wrong, I was never instructed on why I did wrong to the point of real conviction.

Being honest with yourself is an important part of who you are in this world. It's called having good character. This idea I was never taught. There was something missing in my life and I didn't know what is was.

The problem is that I didn't realize that I was actually looking for that *"missing part"* of my life. Since my parents obviously did not have any Christian or religious upbringing, especially my father, therefore I too did not get any type of religious teaching except when they sent me to an Episcopal church when I was young.

The only people in my world at 21 years old were my college friends and professors. The only thing I believed in is what I experienced each day. I lived a life that many students live. It was going to class and attending various forms of social life. I had no family close, so campus life became my family. Hindsight always gives way to revelations as to how you lived in various situations. The thing is, do we learn from hindsight?

One day I was at my college apartment and someone knocked on my door. I lived on the second floor so he had to come up stairs. I opened the door and it was a college aged kid who had a Bible in one hand and began to ask me about God. He said that I should repent from my sins. Well, he almost got a shot in the head with my sins!

This did not exactly go over well with me at the time and I told him that he had to leave because I didn't want to hear any of his religious garbage! He was persistent and kept on telling about sin and God's judgment on me and this world. He just agitated me so much I tried to grab him by his shirt but he backed down a couple of steps so that I could not reach him. After all, I was former military and I had to stand up for what I believed in. I could not afford my ego to be disrupted. I then told him that I was going to call the cops. He was doing what is called *"Bible banging"* and if he had stayed any longer, that is what he was going to get!

So, I walked over to my phone, started to call the police*(the department I would eventually be on!)* but I heard him leave downstairs. This was my first encounter with a Bible banging Christian. This didn't give me a good picture of what a Christian should be like. Later on that day I went to class and had good laughs about it with fellow students.

Music had been a very important part of my life primarily due to the influence of the Beatles and other groups that were emerging during those years. The 1960's and 70's was an explosion of incredible musical talent. I got involved with playing guitar with other people, purchasing good equipment and even started playing in clubs as a one man band. I bought a 4 track recorder and mixed together guitar, drums and bass. I put that onto a cassette tape and used it as backup for me in bars and clubs. I sang out almost every week end at times making some cash for fun. Special events allowed me to play with some well-known artists on campus. Never played at a church though.

I played at many of the college functions like beer bashes, sock hops, and certain college nights. I had a roommate who played out with me. Off campus I played at local clubs, and private parties. It was a lot of fun and I made some money at the same time.

Even though I was getting a monthly check from the VA, I went to work doing some part-time jobs. I worked in Pathmark supermarket behind the deli counter. That was an experience of learning how to cut meat and such. It was also my first experience doing customer service.

I worked at a printing company doing packaging and transporting items. Working UPS was a very physical job. I had to be at work at 4:30 am until 8:30 am where I off-loaded packages from large trailers onto a conveyor belt. That was hard labor for me.

I worked as a shoe salesman in a department store. I even modeled men's clothing at a local men's store. But through all these activities, there was no connection with God or any type of religious organizations. I truly was living a life alone with no parents or brothers or sisters.

I had no mentor except a particular professor and his wife who spoke with me from time to time. There were counselors on campus but I never thought of going to them. I lived day by day. At that time, planning for the future was just not part of my thinking even though I wanted to get into Psychology. It is so important to have some type of mentor to help guide you. It was only God who kept me out of trouble that is so easy to get into on a college campus.

I graduated in 1975 with an AS in psychology and never went on for my BA. Being the class president, I was the speaker at my graduation. I had lost a desire to continue classes primarily because many of the

people I knew were leaving the area. So, I signed up for a couple of classes just to be sociable and to feel a part of the *"scene"*.

While I was involved in college, I also got involved with a CB radio club. CB radio was a big fad during that time and everyone had one. With my experience from the military, I helped them achieve major awards for assisting local and state police in accidents and storms. This club was actually just another avenue for my search to be accepted and loved. I was still playing and singing in clubs and events. This CB club allowed me to meet many political people in the area because we would assist them at their events with sound systems and security. Some of these events were with churches. There I met some people who tried to convey Jesus to me. I was polite, but no way. I see now that meeting people was because I was serving them. This is the gift that God has given me.

At this point in my life, you can see how my life was evolving. I grew up with parents who didn't have relationship with God and didn't attend church. They never read the Bible though my father said he had read it and believed it to be just a story. He had grown up to be an atheist while on the other hand, my mother was brought up Catholic. See any problem there? My mother told me when I came home from the NAVY that I was actually an "Oops" or an unplanned pregnancy and relatives urged my father to have me aborted!

So I made it through High School with no problems other than situations at home. Up until this time, there was no influence of any type of religious teaching. I also never had any thoughts of pursuing any religious teachings. I went through the NAVY and then into college where there was that one time someone had tried to tell me about God and Jesus.

James 1:5

Now if any of you lacks wisdom, he should ask God, who gives to all generously and without criticizing, and it will be given to him.

Chapter Six

Have Gun, Will Travel

Joining the NAVY at 18 years old was the first biggest event in my life. The second was entering college. In 1977, the next big event in my life was about to happen.

One night, I was singing in the pub at the Elks Club. The night was going well and people seemed to enjoy what I was performing. At one of my breaks, a gentleman called me over to his table and introduced himself. He asked me about my background and what I thought I would do in the future. He was the training captain for the Danbury Police Department. He said that because of my NAVY experience, would I like to become a Special Police Officer for the department! He said that *"Specials"* were a part-time job.

It was obvious that my jaw hit the table. He told me what I would need to do and come down to headquarters. Well, my ego was on fire and of course I was at the police department the next day.

At 27, I began my career in law enforcement which would lead me down different paths that I never experienced before. I was entering a world that I only knew from TV. I would be meeting people who loved me because I saved their life and people who wanted to kill me because I arrested them or a relative. There would be very quiet days and days that were nonstop with my life being endangered.

Calls were in shanty type homes and homes that had 4 car garages and theatres in them. I arrested druggies and drunks, husbands and wives, sisters and brothers, aunts and uncles and even a politician or two. But there was no God visible in my life. The closest time I got to God was going on calls to a church.

There was the time I arrested a priest for being totally intoxicated right at his church. It was very embarrassing to the leaders of that church. Then there were shoplifters who came in all sizes and shapes, some were arrested willingly, some with guns and pepper spray. They also came in different occupations including an assistant pastor from a well-known church in the area! He was caught shoplifting! When I came into the security office, he saw me and just cried because he knew me.

So called Christians were a turnoff for me. They didn't act anything like what I presumed a Christian should act like. If there was a God, I was not meeting him on the job. This job was just showing me all the horrors of life and helped me believe that there was no God or Jesus. Church was just for the weak. I thought, maybe my father was right.

Even though I would sing Christmas carols during the season, they were just songs on the radio. It was the same with Easter. The egg laying rabbit was the highlight of the day for me. The closest I got to going to church at that time was doing the crosswalks in front of a church, allowing parishioners to cross going to the service and then after the services. That is about as close as I got to Jesus. We would mimic crossing the people calling them, *"Crosswalks for Jesus."*

I never grew up around any weapons except when I went to summer camp. My father had a .22 rifle which he let me use at the camp. Boy, did I like going down to range to shoot. I remember spending hours there but the counselor would have to tell me to stop because I was using too much ammo. I was about 8 years old at that time.

The first time I owned a gun was when I was sworn in as a Special Police Officer. Specials are part timers and have to supply their own weapons. So I went down to the local gun shop where I was amazed at all the weapons I have never known before. I walked around feeling so ignorant. I explained myself to the shop owner who was very helpful in my innocence.

The first gun I owned was a Trooper Python, 357 magnum. This went along with my inflated ego and my start in law enforcement. This gun shop was just another brick that was added to a wall keeping me away from knowing or hearing anything about the Bible or the truth about having a relationship with God.

Well, I get home with my first handgun and my excitement is flowing from my pores. You have to get the picture of me at this point. I am 27, single, no brothers or sisters, and no parents. I have no one over me telling me what to do. For me, this was ideal! I was now a legal police officer fulfilling my childhood dreams of being a police officer! All those cop shows I had watched and idolized their heroes! I was now among them! A 357 Trooper Python is no small handgun but being in my hand, it was a cannon! It was hard for my head and that gun to get through a doorway together.

I shined that thing every day and practiced my draw to see how fast I could draw. Move over Wyatt Earp! It's called, *"being a rookie"*. But then it occurred to me, how good was I am actually shooting? Could I hit the target? Would I be embarrassed when I first shot? Who would be there to watch me and laugh when I miss the target?

So the day finally came when the training Captain brought me down to the police range downstairs. The range officer was there who showed me how to stand, aim and fire. I spent about six hours on that range. Actually, that day I shot pretty well for a beginner.

The next day I started a 40 hour in-house training which covered many topics. It was a very different experience and a little scary being around all these officers. When you're a rookie, you see all the eyes looking at you knowing that they are critiquing you to see how you behave.

The next week they brought me up to the Mayor's office where I was sworn in officially. This was a giant step in my life which God had planned all along. I would find out years later that the position of police officer is in the Bible! Even though I had my plans each day, it was God who directed my steps.

So now that I'm *"official"*, I need to look official! I took my credit card down to the local uniform store and bought the usual wardrobe officers had in my department. I felt so important. When I got home, of course I had to put the whole thing on and stand in front of the mirror! Was I looking at the real me? Was I actually wearing a real police uniform with a real gun on my side? Angels were probably trying to hold my head together from the ego!

At this point fantasy became reality but reality in my world was still very physical. Looking back as I write this, I'm amazed that I was so independent and trouble could have easily found my doorstep. I had no influence to help me through each day. Whatever came along my way, I just dealt with it the best way I knew how.

What was not coming my way at this time was someone to tell me about God. As a Special Police Officer I basically was a part-time cop who filled in positions that the regular full time guys didn't cover. But at that time there were many open positions during the shifts that allowed me to work at least 40 hours a week and that included private duty like road jobs or events.

Most of those openings were on the 4-12 shift which was very active, in fact often times things were too active and dangerous. But something else came along in my life. I was offered a full time deputy sheriff's job at our superior courthouse which of course my ego jumped right on it. So during the day I was dealing with prisoners and courtroom situations and at night I was patrolling the city streets. Wow, I was carrying two badges! That's ego!

There were no true Christian officers on the force that I was aware of other than the guys who were religiously Catholic. We had a Chaplain from a local church who was a very nice person but I never heard him speak about Jesus to them. It was just an occupation for an established religion. He was always very friendly and was there when the department needed him. That I can say, was a good thing. But where was God? That chaplain never asked me about my relationship with God. God was something people did on Sundays, weddings and funerals. I only believed in what I saw. As the saying goes, believing is seeing I would say. Like Police Officers, I believe ministers should hold a higher standard.

Working at the courthouse was much different than walking a beat. First, I was dressed up in a sport coat and tie. I always had to look presentable in court but it wasn't easy dealing with struggling prisoners wearing those clothes. We weren't allowed to carry weapons of any kind except handcuffs which at times became a weapon for defense. I got to meet criminals of all sorts who absolutely showed me no signs of God. From murders to shoplifters, from rich to poor, from old to young, the variety was plentiful. But again, this just insulated me even more from anything that even came close to God. It helped me become an atheist. Now I can see the battle in my mind as to what reality was with God. There is an enemy who will use anyone and anything to keep you from the truth. It's so incredible how you eyes can be closed to the truth of God.

Law enforcement has always been male dominant and with that comes the perception that because I am a man, I can't cry or show emotions that appear to make me a weak person, no less a weak police officer. Men have always held the appearance of being able to withstand any situations that they encounter. It's called the *"John Wayne syndrome"*. As a police officer, we are supposed to be able to be *"faster than a speeding bullet, more powerful than a locomotive and able to leap tall buildings at a single bound."* (Those were the intro words to the original Superman TV show).

As you become an experienced officer, you find out quickly that you are not Superman! This persona had led to many a suicide whether on the force or not. I thank God that officers and organizations have created many outlets for officers who have to deal with PTSD, stress and suicide.

This image is perpetuated by the media which society falls trap to. Too many people are trying to live the life of Hollywood only to fail in life because it's a life of lies. I was no different. I had my cop shows I watched and had my *"heroes"*. But truth is wrapped up in a different reality that I had not yet witnessed. The only truth I was encountering was the stark reality of bad behavior in a variety of lifestyles. We even had to arrest police officers and judges!

So say the least, no lifestyle is exempt from the reality of committing serious mistakes in life only to fall and fall hard. The saying goes, *"Only the strong survive."* But how do you stay strong? What does it really take to overcome some serious problems we all face in life? Where does God fit into our reality? There are people facing insurmountable problems. They can try to drink them away, or snort them away or even run triathlons to exercise the problems away. Those are temporary Band-Aids that don't relieve problems.

Isn't it strange that as a police officer, my job was to arrest people who would be convicted of a crime yet as a person I was never felt convicted of crimes against God which is called sin. My life to this point never allowed me to feel conviction for the things I did wrong especially to God. Only God can open your eyes to His reality. A criminal knows that they are wrong but are not convicted until they are arrested.

What is your life like? Are you open to any type of religious thinking or do think it is garbage like I did. I thought Jesus was like Santa Claus, nice story but fictional. Are you willing to be open to a truth that maybe you are not aware of, as I was?

We get so caught up in our daily lives that we don't take time out to seek what life is all about until maybe we are on the operating table! Police work can be very intense and totally captivating of the mind. Jesus says that He stands at the door of your thinking waiting for you to seek Him. He cannot force Himself on you for that would not be real love. Think about it. If you have kids, would you want to force yourself on them just to get then to love you?

Chapter Seven

On the Job

In 1980, at the age of 30, I had passed the test for the full time position of police officer and was sworn in with the Danbury Police Department. Not to brag but I came out second place out of the 175 or so who took the test. The person in first place decided to pursue a better offer from another department which then put me in the first place spot. I was elated! This was a big accomplishment for me.

Now life was going to change again for me. Working as a regular officer gets a different respect from the other officers because part time officers usually are not trained as well and don't have the caliber that the full time guys did. But I made the grade! I was proud of what I had accomplished. But now I had to go through the police academy which was conducted by the state police!

It was like the NAVY, you sink or swim! If you flunk out, you go home with your tail between your legs. NOT I! I had to live up to my heroes at the time of *"ADAM 12"*, *"DRAGNET"* and *"CHIPS!"* These are examples of how the media can help develop your belief system. We are a product of what we allow our eyes and ears to experience. You gravitate to the things that you like and motivate you into certain lifestyles. The world is full of things that are sweet and draw you to them. The problem is eating too much sugar can cause cavities!

As I stated in the beginning of this book, these are the situations that occurred in my life and becoming a police officer would be a major life conditioning of the mind. This is why officers commit suicide. Maybe you can't relate to what I went through but you have gone and are going through life situations that affect your thinking about life.

It doesn't matter what department you're talking about, a rookie will always be a rookie and that included me. We are wet behind the ears trying to act like seasoned officers. The other officers know it and so does the public. Fortunately, this symptom doesn't last forever!

Reality begins to shape you into someone different. Police work deals with raw worldly reality at times which can make you question even your existence. This is why officers have a hard time dealing with God and the Bible. God is not a physical reality but His works are! You can't see the air but you can see the result of air through the wind. You can't physically see love but you can see the result of it.

Police Officers see things that the general public doesn't see unless it's on TV or in a movie and but then you're sheltered from the actual experience. Unless you are a robot, this type of life experience will change you, for the good or for the bad.

My first year as a full time Police Officer propelled me into a lifestyle that I was not prepared for. Seeing life from a perspective of evil and violence gave me a different outlook on life. I wondered if there was a God and where was He in all this mess of life. There are times when the *"rose-colored glasses"* need to come off and see life as it really is and in my case, I didn't see God in anything. The Bible says that Satan has blinded the minds of unbelievers to the truth of the Bible. I was an unbeliever because I was never in a situation in which God's truth was told to me.

My first motor vehicle accident I was riding with a senior officer. I was in field training. It was the first *"lights and siren"* call at 60 mph on a secondary road type experience! As we arrived I could see a motorcycle under the trailer of an *"18 wheeler".*

We got out and ran over to the scene where I saw my first decapitation. It was gruesome. I set up the flares and did the traffic direction while the other officer interviewed the trucker. That night I thought a lot about what I had seen and experienced. More of these accidents would be forthcoming in my future. How was God working on me in this first account?

As a police officer, you get to meet people from different walks of life in different situations ranging from a violent encounter to a celebration of sorts. Not all police work is dangerous or violent but there are times when you are assigned to celebrations that are secular or religious in nature. There are assignments of road construction, school dances, sporting events, quiet demonstrations and political events. In these occasions you can meet very nice people and have a great time. These people are another facet of a police experience. But it was the *"religious"* assignments that seemed to have an effect on me. There seemed to be a stirring in me.

Daily experience as a police officer affects you gradually. Unless you're void of thinking, you change and sometimes for the worse. You begin to get the ability to judge character in the various situations of law enforcement. From minor accidents to major crimes, you get insight from the people you have to deal with. It can also make you a critical person.

There are times when you have to make a decision based upon the word of someone rather than physical evidence. Discernment is an ingredient in the recipe of law enforcement. This is how many cases get thrown out of court or the wrong person goes to prison. Your own prejudice can mess up a case because you know that the person is guilty when in fact you don't have evidence to support your conclusion. Isn't that what happened to Jesus . . . no evidence!

One aspect of police work that appeals to officers is that you can never expect each day to be the same. One minute you're sipping you coffee watching traffic at an intersection and the next minute, you're going lights and sirens *(code one for my department)* to a major crime in progress! One day you get no calls and the next day it's call to call to call! One minute you're helping an elderly person cross a street and the next minute you are being shot at.

Sometimes you're involved in an incident with a highly intelligent person and sometimes you're involved with someone that flunked grade school. All these situations affect you just because of the experience. My first year as a full time officer was shock treatment. When I was a *"special"* police officer (part time) I only went to minor calls and accidents. In all this though, rarely did I hear the name of Jesus or reference to God except in foul language.

"On the job", as it is termed, any type of religion was not evidential. After all, we were there to do police work, not socialize! Right! Even on Sundays, the closest I came to God was doing the *"crosswalks for Jesus"* in front of certain churches where we stopped traffic to allow parishioners to cross the street. While I was standing in the middle of the street with my hands out holding traffic back, I wondered about these people who were like sheep going into this building. They didn't seem any different when they came out and there were times when I would see a small domestic argument as they came down the steps!

For me, the best part of doing these crosswalks was that H.Q. couldn't send me on any other calls because I was assigned to them from 8 am to 12 noon! I always had to be there on time because the Deputy Chief went to church and looked for the officer to make sure he was doing the crosswalk!

Of course the only churches we covered were the ones where *"important people"* attended. This was another reason that kept me from seeking God, if he even existed. Politics and hypocrisy are everywhere. Situations like the crosswalks, arresting people who called themselves Christians and arresting priests from denominational churches all hindered me from even thinking about the existence of God and actually pushed me in the opposite direction. How could a God really exist? I couldn't see any signs or evidence of a God. My encounters with so-called Christians were all negative. Then there were the people who did everything they could to shove the Bible down my throat! There was that one time I almost threw someone down my flight of stairs just to get rid of him!

On one occasion, I got called to a church on an *"unruly person"* call. I went into the front of the church where I met a man who was apparently an usher. There was no service going on but about a dozen people were just praying in the pews. This church opened their doors to allow people just to come in and pray. I thought that was a nice thing to do. But this usher brought me around to the side of the sanctuary and walked me up to a particular pew where a man was sitting just praying.

The usher said to me that this man smells so bad that the other people had to move across the aisle and that he doesn't want to leave. I looked at the usher in disbelief! What do you say to that? I asked him, *"You're asking me to remove this man who is praying, not screaming or making any type of disturbance, but you really want me to remove him because he smells?"*

The usher said yes because he is disturbing the rest of the parishioners. This was a homeless man who came into the church to pray. Yes, he did smell but to have him removed by a police officer because he smells? Yes, I had to ask him to leave and he did so without any incident. I brought him outside and apologized to him for their behavior. He was polite and didn't offer any resistance. So I brought him to one of our diners and bought him some breakfast.

Incidents like these are so hypocritical which just killed any desire to want to go to church or read the Bible. If people like what I have mentioned above are what Christians are supposed to be like, it only goes to prove that there is no God because if God did exist, then the people I encounter in a religious situation wouldn't act like they do! How could there be a God who supposedly was a God of love allow these people to be like this if they were following their God? There was no rationale for me to understand my perplexity of these situations.

There was an incident where I was sent to a department store for a shoplifter. When I arrived, the store security officer explained what had happened and let me review the video tape of the security system. I then went into the room where the suspect was and read him the Miranda rights. I took his wallet to retrieve ID and saw that he was an assistant pastor at a large well known church in the area!

Here was another example of a Christian that didn't practice what was preached. I said to him, *"And you're a pastor!"* He began to cry. I thought to myself, another *'Jesus freak'* hypocrite!

Prior to getting on the force full time in 1980, life seemed to be just great with working 2 jobs in law enforcement, and just enjoying my lifestyle at the time. But once *"on the job"* full time, life changed primarily because of shift rotation and working holidays.

An officer becomes disconnected with the *"normal"* daily working timeline of 9-5, Monday through Friday and weekends and holidays off. You see, law enforcement, firefighters and medical people all are available 24/7 and someone has to work the night shifts and someone has to work holidays and weekends. These shifts change you physically and mentally and not for the better.

Your body may not get used to the midnight hours and mentally you can get marooned from friends because they have a different set of hours than you have. The lifestyle of first responders can absolutely change your morals and any decency in you unless you have something strong to hold onto.

The *"Big 3"* as I call them, cops, firemen and medical see the worst factions of life. We see things that the general public will never see and no one should ever see them! When you see bodies blown apart, decapitations, bodies burned to a crisp, children raped it is no wonder that a person would ask, *"Is there a God?"* Why would a God allow all this horrendous activity to occur if he is a God of love? It doesn't make natural sense!

I thought people going to church were fulfilling an obligation like sheep led to the slaughter. I remember sitting with someone, mocking them for believing in Jesus. I told them that I could believe that he really did exist as a teacher who wrote a good book of great moral values. But I couldn't believe in an entity that created the whole universe and picked this tiny little planet from all the other solar systems for his plan of action!

If I didn't see it, I didn't believe it. That was my philosophy at the time. This based upon my life so far and especially now that I had just become a full time police officer. My experiences from school, the NAVY, college and now law enforcement combined to make me believe that only reality was what I could physically see and touch especially a good steak and a beer.

"*The best laid schemes of mice and men*". This is from Robert Burns' poem, "*To a Mouse*". This is where John Steinbeck wrote the famous book, "*Of Mice and Men*", featuring George and Lennie who together decide to create plans for the future. The problem is that life happens and George and Lennie meet people who change their life forever. It's a sad ending novel.

The overall concept of this book can reveal the things that happen in all of our lives. We make plans to do things from time to time but sometimes life gets in the way and we have to switch course and go on. We meet people along the way who can influence us in good and bad directions. Sometimes, we don't realize that we are being conditioned into thinking in a certain manner. We are influenced everyday whether you know it or not.

Temptations always come our way in various forms each of which we can follow or use discernment to do something else. Thus you may think life is great and you have plans for the future but storms come in everyone's life no matter what their lifestyle is.

Vivian Greene wrote, *"Life isn't about waiting for the storms to pass . . . It's about learning to dance in the rain."* Here's the question: how do you dance in the rain? I know now that God was orchestrating my life but it was right after I got on the force that things began to change. Rain happens but not all the time. Isn't the sun always out but can be hidden by clouds? What clouds do you need to clear from your life to be able to see the truth? What gets rid of the clouds in our lives is the time we spend in prayer seeking God to remove them. He doesn't always remove them but goes through it with us to give us peace in the moment.

Jeremiah 29:11

For I know the plans I have for you"—this is the Lord's declaration—"plans for your welfare, not for disaster, to give you a future and a hope.

Chapter Eight

The Music Store

I don't remember what day of the week it was in 1981, but I was on my way to a local music store to look at some guitars and amps. I loved music and enjoyed my guitar. This was a store that I could spend hours in just enjoying the atmosphere. There were times *"famous"* band members would come in like the time I met Felix Cavalier from the Young Rascals! That was a memory!

Anyway, as I drove into the parking lot of the store, another car had just pulled in also. I got out and headed towards the door, this lady approached me who was in that other car. She was a local female evangelist, Grace DiBicarri, who sang and produced concerts for her ministry called Grace and Vessels. She came right up to me and began to tell about Jesus Christ. Immediately, I said to myself, *"Oh no another Jesus freak!"* But I was polite and stopped to listen to her. Flesh is flesh and it can rule you! So I listened to her and for the first time I heard about God like I never heard it before. There was something in her manner of speaking about God that made me listen and want to hear more. I was curious but not curious enough to keep on listening to her. The music coming from the store was more attractive to me. So I said good bye and went into the store and so did she.

Inside, the owners knew her because of the frequency that she was in the store. I didn't pay attention to what she was doing and went about what I wanted to look at. I finished after a while and decided to leave for home. As I went out, so did she. Walking outside, she said to me that she wanted to invite me to one of her concerts. I said maybe and went home only to forget the whole incident.

As with, *"Of Mice and Men,"* you can make your plans but situations and people occur in your life that you didn't expect to happen. This is how God works. He has a plan for everyone and I was no exception. Meeting this lady at the music store was no accident. Of course as an atheist I would argue you that point. But God knows what he is doing and brings the right people in your path of life at the right time. Of course, you don't know that at the time. This lady planted seeds of thought that would be watered by other people who would eventually cross my path.

As time went on, through daily police work and social activities, I got to meet different types of people as I have explained previously. Sometime during the spring of 1981 after meeting this lady at the music store, I got invited to a special breakfast at the local Holiday Inn.

Now understand my life style at the time. I lived the lifestyle of many who smoke and drank except I smoked a pipe. I wasn't a *"real"* drinker but had my beers once in a while and hated the thought of being drunk because of my parents' alcoholism. As a police officer, I hated doing DUI stops. I was a social drinker which means I only drank because I was out and others were drinking at the time and I wanted to look sociable.

So picture this. I am dressed in a turtleneck shirt and a corduroy sport coat and jeans looking like a professor with a pipe. I go into the Holiday Inn and inquire the whereabouts of this breakfast. I am shown what room it's in and head towards the door which is open. As I get to the  door, the guy who invited me is standing there and grabs my hands and says, *"Bob, welcome! I have a table for you over here. I'm glad you could make it!"*

So I'm starting to sweat because this room is filled to the max with about 250 people. I sit down at a table with about 6 other people who all seemed very friendly. They say hello and I say hello back to them. Well, we all get served a standard hotel breakfast and not much talk is happening at my table which was okay with me because when people find out that you're a police officer, all the complaints about their tickets seem to come out.

I begin to look at some of the literature that is at the table. I am at a breakfast of the Full Gospel Businessmen's Fellowship International! From that moment I start to sweat! How did I get here! What am I doing here! How did I get roped into coming to a Jesus freak show?

So I'm sitting there and I take out my pipe. Now understand there is NO ONE smoking in this big room! I light up and if you have ever seen a pipe smoker, a lot of smoke can be made! So I'm sitting there at the table and no one is saying anything like, *"smoking is not allowed"* but no one said anything! I look around and now I feel totally out of place. I'm thinking, how do I get out of this place without being noticed? The problem is, you can't miss me because of my pipe smoke! Try to picture a cloud of smoke hovering over my head! Also, there was no ash tray to put my pipe!

The music stops and there seems to be a small break where people mingle a lot. I'm about to get up and leave when the guy who invited me comes over and says that he has someone he wants me to meet! That's just great! How do I become invisible! So I say, sure and he calls one the main guys from the head platform over to my table where I am sitting.

This guy comes over and shakes my hand as he introduces himself. He says, *"Hi. My name is Alan. It's good to meet you. I've heard a lot about you. I'm a Bethel police officer and I understand you're a Danbury police officer."* I said yes. *(Bethel was the town right next to Danbury)* By this time, the sweat is running like a river down my back. The sweat ran down my brow and into my eyes which fogged my eyesight. He then said that he'd like to get together sometime but he had to get back up on the dais. I gave him my phone number. He said not to worry about the pipe smoke. It doesn't matter to us and he went back up.

I don't remember much about the guest speaker and what he had to say. All I remember is that I was surrounded by a batch of Jesus people with their arms raised singing about Jesus! The head guy said put your hands up and praise God. Not me! There is no God. If they want to believe in some God, that's okay with me. But what about this cop from Bethel? What do I do with him? What has he heard about me? How can he carry a gun and call himself a Christian? Don't they believe in not killing, I thought isn't one of the commandments: *"Thou shalt not kill?"* That's all I need in my life is a Bible banging cop trying to tell me how to live! I really didn't want to hear from him at all. Later on I would find out that was a mistranslation. It should read *"Thou Shalt not Murder".* Big difference.

A couple of weeks go by and he calls me. He wants to know what shift I'm on. I tell him midnights so he thinks I won't have time to meet him because when you're on mids, you sleep during the day. Therefore, we couldn't meet! Right? Nope. He says he's on mids also and wants to meet up at the border between our towns.

So that night I'm on patrol and he calls me and says he's free right now and meet at the border. I said okay and we pull up side by side as you have seen police cars do at times. Yes, cops do meet like that but it's not only for chit-chat. Many times officers meet to exchange important information that they don't want over their radios because of the general public can listen to police conversations on their scanner. We have civilians show up at crime scenes trying to *"assist"* officers and getting in the way.

So, we're sitting side by side talking "cop shop". After a while he pulls the question. How did you like the breakfast? I go, um, um it was good. The food was good. Nice music. So, he's smiling knowing I feel uncomfortable about the topic. He asks me if I go to church and I said I did when I was 10 years old. I don't want anything to do with it. He says I have something for you.

He picks up a small book and says this is a Bible. I immediately say no thanks! He says look, here take it, it's free. I said no thanks and you can put that Bible where the sun doesn't shine! I told him I appreciate the thought but no thanks and drove off. This cop is not getting involved with any Jesus people! I deal with reality not some religious people! I took off and was bombarded with thoughts for the rest of the shift.

I could hardly finish my reports because I kept thinking about this Jesus stuff and a cop who calls himself a Christian. I then remembered that lady from the music store! Am I getting into some type of cult? Why are these types of people coming into my life? My life would now be changing in a different direction than I had initially planned.

As with many other occupations, police work can become very overwhelming. It's the type of lifestyle that can control most of your thinking especially if you really enjoy the job. It also depends on your location, what type and the quality of leadership, and the direction of the department. Depending on your locale, experience in this field can actually get you to think thoughts that you never imagined before! There were times, as many officers have asked themselves, *"Why am I here?"* You see and experience things that no one should ever experience and you question what life is really about.

The problem with most people is that they are controlled by the life they lead which doesn't require that you look at yourself honestly and to seek why you are on this planet. This occupation will sometimes force you into questioning what life is about and where are you going. Consistent thinking in this vein can lead to depression and then suicide. If you don't know who you are and why you do what you do, then desperation can set in leading you to think that there is no reason for you to be alive.

When I first wore a badge in the late 70's, I was enjoying life as a single who hung with some fun people. They were always encouraging me which gave me reason to go on each day. I was controlled by my environment and the people I chose to be around. But at that time, there was no one telling me about the Bible or God. Even though these people that I was around where good people, they never mentioned anything about going to church or anything related to Jesus Christ except in vulgar manner.

There is a persona that runs through much of law enforcement, especially lately with all the *"anti-cop"* events, that says, *"us against them"*. When you put on that uniform, badge and gun, you step into a world that is structured differently than the rest of the world.

First, you work rotating shifts, holidays and your wedding anniversary if you can't get off. Second, as I have said before, you are in a very physical, graphic world that most officers are not trained to deal with. Third, you still have a foot back in the *"normal people"* world where you have bills to pay, kids to send to school and a relationship to keep functioning on a happy level. This is a formula for disaster because your body does need to get proper sleep and your mind does need peace at times in order to function and move on to the next scenario. So where does an officer find a balance in this occupation?

The divorce rate is extremely high as is the suicide rate. It really is a matter of your lifestyle and how you grew up for the most part. There are always exceptions to the rule but your basic foundation that your parents laid into you whether they did it intentionally or not is what you fall back on later in your life unless major changes affect you in some manner.

A major problem is the facade that police work has established since its inception and that is officer cannot show weakness because they are a public figure and on the side of law, especially being a male. Of course today, women are now in law enforcement but still that persona of being and looking strong at all times still is in the forefront. If you bring in the topic of God or the Bible you are shunned and rejected because many see religion as a weakness having to go to church like sheep.

For me, even though my father was an atheist, he never shoved his philosophy down my throat. On the other hand my mother never pushed her Catholicism at me either. God was just not brought up in conversation except when Sunday came around and they brought me to an Episcopal church. Someday maybe God will show me how they compromised their beliefs so differently and brought me to a church.

Trust is a word that is thrown around every day in every type of situation you can imagine. Ask people what the definition is and you will hear many different answers. When you *"Google"* the definition, here's what you get: *"firm belief in the reliability, truth, ability, or strength of someone or something."*

Sometimes trust is automatic and sometimes trust must be earned. Trust is usually based upon experience where you can rely on that person or something. In my world, I didn't seek trust in someone or something but just accepted what I was faced with at the time.

I never questioned whether my gun would fire or whether the chair I was going to sit in would break. It's easy to trust in something you see and are familiar with. But what about having trust in something you can't see?

As an atheist, I only trusted in things I could see and touched my senses. An atheist trusts in the substantiation of valid physical proof and this is what I believed in. Police officers deal with the physical and mental but not the spiritual. There is no spirituality in a courtroom proving your case. Yet in many courtrooms the USA Motto is on the wall, *"In God We Trust"*. It's also on the dollar bill.

I was not a card carrying member of an atheist group but just rejected the notion of an all-powerful God that I couldn't see. This was because my world consisted, at the time, of people who didn't talk about the Bible or God as if they were real.

I never encountered anyone in the NAVY who remotely sounded like a Christian. I had one person in college who attempted to tell me about Jesus but all I did was call the cops on him to get him out of my doorway! Now on the police force, my first 4 years I had no one ever tell me the truth about the Bible.

Jeremiah 29:12,13

You will call to Me and come and pray to Me, and I will listen to you. You will seek Me and find Me when you search for Me with all your heart.

Chapter Nine

NYPD

During 1982, I don't remember the specific dates and times, but I had been invited to attend various Christian events most of which I didn't attend. But there was one event that I went to at a church that was for *"young adults"*. Now I was still smoking my pipe at the time. I went in and met some of the people attending. There were about 25 all looking *"clean"* but here I am smoking my pipe. I must have stood out like a sore thumb!

Anyway, they were all very nice and never pushed any Bible stuff on me which I thought was strange because that is what I expected! No, they were polite and actually spoke to me with respect. They asked about my police work and said that they were glad that I had come. We watched an *"end times"* movie which I thought was ridiculous because it was not anywhere near Hollywood quality.

I don't remember the title but it must have had a 50 cent budget to make. I sat there after the movie just listening to their discussion. The Bethel police officer that I had met sometime before was there also approached me and said that he was glad that I had come. He wanted to get together again and I said call me which he did not call for some time. There are times on the job that you get to meet officers from other departments because of cases that you work on.

Well, I got to meet an NYPD officer on a case that the suspect had done crimes in NYC and Danbury. After we had discussed the case and worked on it for some time, He asked me if I believed in God. Totally taken by surprise, I stumbled at my answer expressing doubt in a God of the universe. He then invited me down to the Bronx for a special *"meeting"* with a bunch of NYPD officers. They were meeting at a church which raised my eyebrows. He had known that I videotaped events and asked me if I would tape this meeting. I said sure thinking how great it would be to hang with some NYPD guys!

To say the least, this event would radically change my present thinking about NYPD officers and God. If you know anything about the Bronx, it's not your easy place to get around unless you are from there. I'm glad I left very early because I got lost.

I am also a punctual type person and if you know about us punctual types, we're never late! We are never on time either because we are always early. We cringe at the thought of being late and do anything to get to a place early. If I have a doctor's appointment at 10 am, I am sitting in the parking lot at least 20 minutes beforehand! It's just something we punctual people do.

Anyway, I got down to this church in the Bronx, got my gear out and walked into this old building which used to be some kind of small factory. I met some officers at the door who were so friendly to me; you thought that we had been brothers! I took my equipment and walked through the hallway and entered into a large room like a small gym. I had heard music coming inside but did not think anything about it until I came to the door of this large room. I looked in and could not believe what my eyes were looking upon. I just stood there trying to do a check on the reality of my situation. My life was about to take a turn in the map of my life.

As I mentioned before, in law enforcement you can get a chance to meet officers from all over the country depending upon the case you're dealing with. NYPD officers have been the most desired department because of their great reputation as well as all the movies using NYPD. So they become somewhat of a symbol of what officers should do and act like. Most police uniforms for many years were copied from NYPD uniforms. They are a status symbol.

So, I enter this hall. On the right were the officers that I was told would be there for this *"meeting"* which didn't take but a few seconds to know that this was not a meeting that I was expecting especially with the ALL the people that were in this hall. The officers on the right were all in uniform from a Captain down to patrolman. There were about 50 of them. On the left side of the room were men all dressed in orange outfits. Guess what they were? Convicts! Yes, criminals, bad guys, and the people we arrest! I didn't know what to say or do.

In front of everyone was a stage with a man singing to a recording. His name was Alvin Slaughter. What was happening at this location is commonly called *"having church"*. This was called a *"Cops and Cons"* event. Everyone had their hands up praising Jesus and singing along. If there was some way of shrinking through the floor at that time, I would have done so but instead I just started to set up my video camera and equipment.

There are no real words that I can express as to how I was feeling at that time. Mixed emotions would not do as how I felt. I didn't know what to think having never been in a situation like this. Cops to my right and cons to my left! If that was not enough, when the music stopped, the MC told everyone to greet one another!

The cops and cons began hugging each other! That should have made headlines! I began to think that I needed an aspirin! I thought I was in an episode of the *"Twilight Zone!"* This was not a skit on Saturday Night Live!

Well, I recorded the event and wished that I had kept a copy. But it was good that I met all the officers and felt accepted among them. We all ate together and then I went home. You could say that day I saw my first miracle of cops and convicts hugging each other. I met one of the officers who was with an organization called International Cops for Christ. He invited me to their meetings which later on I would eventually go. But for now I would be doing a lot of thinking as to what I had just witnessed. God will work in your life when you don't expect it. He knows what is going to happen because he had a plan for my life.

My life now has had a major influence of which I was not expecting in any manner. As you grow up, you hear and see people's lives being changed for the good and the bad depending on their circumstances. You watch the news and see tragedies all around the world. As a police officer, you go on calls not to celebrate situations but to eradicate bad ones. Sometimes you make friends and sometimes you make enemies. Each day that goes by, something enters your life and changes it even if it is very small and unnoticeable. Acquiescence comes into play because of life's routines and the situations we find ourselves in.

This was a major event in my life meeting these police officers in New York. I saw one thing but my mind could not handle it because of my belief system. How could police officer sworn to uphold the law, arrest criminals and then go to church with them?

Something does not compute! My life had been one of *"seeing is believing"* yet I know what I saw. The experience was too overwhelming to just forget because it involved my job. Usually when hands go up, it's only the criminals but at this event cops and criminals were raising their hands to God! It's like I wanted to hit the rewind button just to watch it again to confirm what I had witnessed. This event I believe occurred in the spring of 1982. Summer was coming and so was the beginning of the end of my belief system that I had stood upon all my life.

My daily life began to change slowly in that I began to look at life and started to ask questions which never entered my mind before. I had never questioned life before even though some of the most horrible situations as a police officer would make anyone ask why this did happen.

Part of investigating incidents whether it is an auto accident, burglary or homicide, is that you have to interview people to get their testimony of what had occurred. Based upon evidence and their testimony, you usually come to a conclusion that would explain the incident. But now I'm listening to people who claim that there is a God who sent his son down here on earth to *"save us"*. I ask, save us from what?

Good police work is not just based upon gathering evidence, your training, listening to testimony but it's the ability to perceive the truth through your intuition. Most officers rely upon the old statement, *"If it looks like a duck, smells like a duck, quacks like a duck, then it's a duck, but nope not always!"* Remember the story about the wolves in sheep's clothing?

Sometimes the sheep's clothing is professionally made! Ever buy some fresh apples, bite into one that looks great only to find inside part of it was rotten! So now people are sending me audio tapes of testimonies from people who became Christians who had a conversion that would make a Hollywood movie! And some did!

I listened to a man by the name of Bob Ehler who was a Florida cop in two towns. He was known as the, "*Catch Me Killer*". He was sentenced to prison for murdering someone but was released extremely early defying all odds. Look it up on Google. As summer was approaching, I got invited to go to different events including church.

When I was at work, I began to see my investigations differently even if it was a minor motor vehicle accident. It's hard to explain but I would ask myself why are these things are happening in life. I never did that before. I just did what I had to do to accomplish my work. I started to go to a church and met some great people who were just ordinary people like me.

Sometimes you have preconceived notions about what Christians should be like and I did have those notions. But these people came from various walks of life and jobs. They would talk to me about Jesus as if they knew him like a next door neighbor, someone you could talk to anytime. I couldn't help but believe what they were saying because they seemed so genuine.

Chapter Ten

PTA

During the summer of 1982, I met a couple of guys from church who approached me and asked if I would consider starting a *"gospel"* band. Now the only *"gospel"* music I knew was Mahalia Jackson who was a black gospel singer called the *"Queen of Gospel"*. There was no way I was going to get involved in that. They had come to me because they had heard that I played guitar and had sang in a variety of places. I told them no thanks but they would come to me once in a while asking again.

So, one day I broke down and said let's get together and talk about this idea. It was my *"PTA"* so to speak. Understand that at this time, I was a non-believer. I only said yes to appease them. After all, I was going to their church once in a while and I didn't want me to look bad. You have to understand at this point, I was still a *"top 40's"* man listening to the latest groups. All the groups I grew up with like the Beatles, the Stones, Simon and Garfunkel were still my favorite music groups to listen to. Even today, they still are extremely popular.

About a week later on a Sunday afternoon I went over to one of the guys homes with the *"I'm not getting involved in this"* attitude. We sat around for a short while telling me about who they were individually. I found out that we were all Beatle *"freaks"* and talked sometime about the group.

Finally I asked them what this gospel group idea was about. They said they wanted to create a Christian band. I asked what kind of Christian music you are talking about. They said it was like the music that was playing in the background. Now, I had not really listened to that background music that was playing because it was like a rock group or pop style music.

I hadn't thought about it at all until they pointed it out. They were playing music from Amy Grant and the Imperials, all Contemporary Christian music. I had never heard of *"contemporary"* Christian music! After all, I was a top 40's kind of guy. Christian music never entered my life until now. They played for me a number of artists who had a very contemporary sound which I actually liked. I said now that I had an idea of what they were looking to do, I would take some time and think about it.

Well, by now my life was really messed up trying to make sense of all these testimonies especially from Christian police officers and now these people that I have been meeting for the past six months or so.

That Sunday night as I laid in my bed starting to talk to the ceiling as if someone was listening. I would say things like, *"If there is a God, I have been lied to about life, is there something that I have not been told right in front of me?"* What actually happens when you die?

Questions like these plagued me that night and the next few days. Getting into my police cruiser seemed different somehow as if everything was going to be OK.

On Wednesday, I was off from work and decided to get my guitar out and see if I could play some of this music that they had been talking about. Since I had no tapes of those groups at home, I opened a musician's sheet music book that was loaded with secular songs but in the back was a section of *"religious"* music sheets.

I went to that section and pulled out some old gospel songs and tried to play them like a contemporary style. After an hour, it just didn't come together. Understand that at this point in my life I had never written any songs except one night several years earlier, while watching Johnny Carson, I actually wrote a song called, *"Change your Life"*. Don't ask why I was playing my guitar and watching Johnny Carson. There is no explanation. Can you believe that? Was God trying to show me something that night?

So I began to put some chords together trying to create a song and four hours later I had written six songs about Jesus! I could not believe what I had done! It just flowed out of me. I didn't tell anyone about this. I was kind of shocked and began to really come to grips about all this Jesus stuff. The wall that I had created all my life was crumbling. For the first time, I began to think that God was real and that he did have a son called Jesus but I was not yet ready to give in. Your mind can create a lot of doubts about anything and God was one of them. Remember, *"Seeing is believing"*.

The next night I got a call from that Bethel Police Officer inviting me over for dinner the following Saturday night. Later on down the road, I found out that this was an ambush meaning that some people from the church had set this up and were praying for me in another room.

Dinner was good and we finally got around about the topic of God and Jesus Christ. Now understand that I am sitting with a group of people and opposite me is this officer. He would ask me questions that I could not answer like if there is no battery inside of you, what keeps your heart beating since you have no control over it? But he was very calm and polite but persistent as I was persistent in trying to defend my belief system which obviously was being smashed before me. Everyone left around 11 PM and he and I talked until 4 am! As I went home I said, *"God if you are real and everything that I have been hearing is true, then please show me."* I went home and slept like a rock.

The next day was Sunday, September 19, 1982. During the day, I thought about what had been happening to me and decided to seek the reality of God because inside of me knew now that there was a God. I could just feel it. I can't explain it in words.

I went to the evening service and spoke with the pastor before the service telling him that I wanted to give my life to God. Service started and the music lasted for about a half hour.

The pastor then said to the congregation that someone decided that he wanted to give his life to Christ. I stood up and began to walk down the aisle to the altar as everyone began to clap and cheer me on! I was sweating like a flood. I did not know what to expect. Me, a cop walking to an altar to turn my life over to a God that I did not know!

When I got to the altar, I stood in front of the pastor. He asked me to **put my hands up** in the air. He then laid his hand on my shoulder. Just when he did, a batch of people came running over to me and did the same! I was just arrested by God! You could say that I was taken into His custody!

Now, if you're a police officer reading this, what would you do if a batch of people laid their hands on you? Yep, but I didn't! Here I am with a Beretta 9mm on my side, under my jacket, with people laying their hands all over me and praying in some unknown language! I could have passed out! BUT something happened to me. It's hard to explain it in English but I had such a peace come over me and felt extremely calm. I even began to cry for unknown reasons.

When the praying stopped they all hugged me and I turned around. I looked up and there was that cop jumping up and down with his hands in the air! He came over to me and called me *"brother"*! I choked up because no one ever called that! I went and sat down and listened to the rest of the service with a new way of thinking, is the best way I can explain it. An usher handed me a red Bible for me to keep. At this point it's hard to explain what I was feeling because I had never felt this way. I felt like a burden was lifted off of me and felt free. From there on, life has never been the same. I was a different person. By the way, yes, we formed a

contemporary Christian band called the *"Good News Band"* and played out in many churches and public events. We actually made an album!

Yes, life changed radically but what can you expect? I had become a *"born again Christian."* The next day I was working day shift and everyone could see that I was acting differently. I was happy and smiling. That wasn't normal to be that happy with a group of cops around. But after roll call and we all went outside to our cruisers, they saw me put that red Bible on my dashboard! Oh, yes, it began.

Chapter Eleven

QUE PASA¿

OK, so now what? The next day I am doing day shift. I go into the locker room humming some song I don't remember. One of the guys comes over to me and says. *"Que pasa¿"*. He's not Spanish but it was a statement that is popular instead of asking *"what's up?"*. I am standing in front of my locker and as I am putting on my duty belt, I tell him I went to church last night. And of course he comes out and says, "WHOA!. You went to church on a Sunday night!". I said yes and I went down to the altar and gave my life to God. Well, the laughter couldn't have been any louder! We then went into roll call where he told everyone there that I had become *"one of those born agains!"*. *"Faubel found God!"* He says! I'm sure I was red faced but sat there quietly. The Sergeant comes in and the officer now tells the sergeant! Well, the sergeant joins in exclaiming that, *"We now have a minister in our presence!"*. A minister? Well, to say the least, life changed drastically for me from that day on.

Aside from the guys trying to make fun of me, what exactly did happen to me from then on? How would I look at my occupation knowing that I carry a weapon that can kill someone? How would I react to the situations that still faced me on a daily basis as a Police Officer?

I attended church every week and met some great people. First of all let me explain that just because someone is a Christian, doesn't mean that they are perfect or that they don't have some skeletons in their closet. Everyone has things in their lives. Plus having Christian friends does not mean they won't back stab you sometime. People are people and perfect and they have their hang ups but the goal is to allow God to change you and give you strength to overcome any challenge.

Guys would throw it in my face using the Bible scripture, *"Doesn't the Bible say that thou shall not kill?"* Initially I did have trouble with that but after studying the scripture, it means that *"Thou shall not MURDER"*. Different idea when you get into the Bible and find out what it really means and what they meant when they wrote it.

As time went on, I began to see not only my job in a different light but life in general had a different meaning. I was not harsh anymore or dogmatic in different situations. I now saw life as God was running things but that Satan was creating some much confusion and anger in life. When you go to college, you don't learn everything in one day and graduate the next day. It takes time to read and study the Bible. Just like we had to read and understand our motor vehicle laws manual in order to apply it to the situations we encountered. We had to learn the book on criminal laws for us to arrest people and apply the proper law to that case or application for a warrant. It's the same with the Bible.

When I would go to a domestic assault case, I now understood that this case and all the rest are created by the evil in this world which gave me a better understanding on how to handle the people involved. I did what I had to do to make the arrest and becoming a Christian never hindered me in any way but gave me a different perspective. I actually had more compassion on the people in the cases I was involved in. I did what I was hired for but in a different light now.

In the book of Romans, God says that this job of law enforcement is required to enforce the laws that are in place and that if someone breaks that law, they should be afraid of the consequences. God knew what He was doing. He knew that man was corrupt because of Satan. It's when you understand that, it will give you strength to know that God is on your side IN EVERYTHING!

Through the years and all the cases, the guys saw how I reacted in various situations and believe me, they were watching to see if I would make a mistake! Do you know anyone watching you to see if you screw up?

A real Christian cop sees his job as fulfilling the obligation that God has placed on him and not doing it for self gratification. He sees himself as a servant and that is exactly what a cop should be. The major problem that is in law enforcement is the stereotype of being a cop like the ones you see on TV. That image has been around for so long and it causes so many problems all the way to suicide. If you're Police officer, then you know that to be true.

I am proud to say that it was God who got me through so many bad scenarios. There were times that the only answer to how I came out alive, was God! No argument! I had guys come to me privately asking me questions anything from what a scripture meant to explain what was Jesus all about and to pray for them!

I could do "shop talk" all day but the bottom line is that having gave my life to Jesus Christ, changed my life and my occupation where as I mentioned before that the guys started an FOP chapter, that the only person they could think of out of all 150 officers to fill the Chaplain's position, was me. Why? It was God opening that door for me to tell them about what Jesus did for them. It was a witness.

What happened to me will happen to you if you decide to turn your life over to God through His son, Jesus Christ. It's not religion God wants but a direct relationship with him!

The teasing and harassment followed me for a long time. But God was good to me and showed me how to have the strength to get through any problem that I faced especially on the job. I saw things differently and acted differently. I could not put that Bible down and eventually went to the local Christian Bookstore and bought my own Bible. I absorbed the words in the book. Reading those words changed me forever. I'm not going to preach here but I'm simply saying that once I gave my life to Christ, life changed for the best. Yes, I still had trials confronting me but now I had a different way of handling them.

My job as a police officer changed because I saw the occupation in a different light. The Bible says that this position is ordained by God to fight evil and that people should be aware of the punishment for breaking laws. God knew that evil would create problems and that law enforcement was necessary.

For the rest of my career, I served as a Christian Police Officer. Believe me, when you make that decision, the people you work with notice it right away. Some people accept it and others don't but that did not persuade me at all. It just proved even more the truth about what was in that Bible.

After I gave my life to Jesus Christ, God opened up doors and I got involved in a number of Men's ministries in my church and outside. I met other officers from other departments and we formed Connecticut Cops for Christ. I had speaking engagements with the Full Gospel Businessmen's Fellowship International and traveled to different states giving my testimony of what God was doing in my life.

Prior to getting off the PD, I worked part time at my church producing the TV show, creating graphics, and producing much of the layout work for printed materials. I also did much of the photography whenever needed. I eventually worked full time there as a *"Media Pastor"* producing the TV show.

I became a local director for Promise Keepers in my area and organized trips to their events. I received an invitation for me and another officer to appear on international Christian TV, Trinity Broadcasting Network, to give our testimonies. I also received another invitation to appear again out in California at their main station. The local TBN station asked me many times to come over and talk about witchcraft and Satanism since Cops for Christ had been putting on presentations about Halloween each year. God opens many doors when you work for Him!

I retired from my department in 2001 because I was injured in an accident with my cruiser. Four years later my sergeant, Johnny Krupinsky, calls me asking if I would be the Chaplain for the Fraternal Order of Police chapter that the department was starting. I said yes but asked him why he was asking me. He said that out of all the officers on the force, they couldn't think of anyone who would do the job in the best way! I was so honored!

So, I got my Theology degree, became an ordained minister and police chaplain and now serve as a Chaplain wherever I go. I also became a Chaplain for my department. Life goes on each day and the clock keeps moving forward. There is no "*undo*" button in life. God gave us the ability to make choices in life and like anyone who reads this; I have made some bad decisions.

We are all fallible, susceptible for making mistakes. It's when we get honest with ourselves and admit our faults that we begin to face reality that we will not live forever. The worlds' thinking and ways do not want you to think about dying but dying happens. God will not force his way into your life but wants you to come to him in the same way you would want your children to come to you in love.

You have the choice of seeking God as I did and as so many other people have done. It's not religion that God wants but he wants a relationship with you. He calls to you all the time but you have to have ears to listen and be willing to listen. He puts people and events in your life to get you to open your eyes to his existence. Let me say this finally, that as a police officer I had to come to conclusions based upon facts and testimonies of the people involved. I had to make a choice about the outcome.

God had a warrant for my arrest because I sinned against him. I put my hands up and surrendered to him. But he sent Jesus to pay for what I had done. You have read my testimony and the facts that occurred in my life. Therefore I am asking you to come to a conclusion about God and his son Jesus Christ because he has a warrant for you. Just ask him into your life now and surrender.

Law enforcement has always been male dominant and with that comes the perception that because I am a man, I can't cry or show emotions that appear to make me a weak person, no less a weak police officer. Men have always held the appearance of being able to withstand any situations that they encounter.

As a police officer, we are supposed to be able to be *"faster than a speeding bullet, more powerful than a locomotive and able to leap tall buildings at a single bound."* (Those were the intro words to the original Superman TV show.) As you become an experienced officer, you find out quickly that you are not Superman!

This persona had led to many a suicide whether on the force or not. This image is perpetuated by the media which society often falls trap to. Too many people are trying to live the life of Hollywood only to fail in life because it's a life of lies. I was no different. I had my cop shows I watched and had my *"heroes"*. But the truth is wrapped up in a different reality that I had not yet witnessed. The only truth I was encountering was the stark reality of bad behavior in a variety of lifestyles. We even had to arrest police officers and judges!

So to say the least, no lifestyle is exempt from the reality of committing serious mistakes in life only to fall and fall hard. The saying goes, *"Only the strong survive."* But how do you stay strong? What does it really take to overcome some serious problems we all face in life?

There are people facing insurmountable problems. They can try to drink them away, or snort them away or even run triathlons to exercise the problems away. Those are temporary Band-Aids that don't relieve problems. Yet there are some who just walk through problems with no sweat. So the face of *"Machoism"* has been prevailing and I was a subject of that kingdom. Isn't it strange that as a police officer, my job was to arrest to get them convicted of a crime yet as a person I was never felt convicted of crimes against God which is called sin. My life to this point never allowed me to feel conviction for the things I did wrong especially to God. A criminal knows that they are wrong but are not convicted until they are arrested.

In 2006, I was divorced. It tore me apart and hurt my kids. I went through an experience that many police officers go through because of the job. It's very easy to point your finger as to who was at fault and the person who points the finger usually is part of the problem. It also was the year of my first heart attack.

Today I am married to a wonderful woman. Together we have 4 adult children from previous marriages who all have their own lives now. We have given our lives to God to serve Him with the gifts that He has given to us.

Chapter Twelve

What does God want with You?

People used to think the world was flat and maybe some still do. This was based upon what they saw physically. Look at the news today and you will see people getting mad because they saw this 15 second video and made a decision on that video without the facts or the whole story.

How many police officers have been crucified because of how those people reacted to a short video? The media only shows what it wants you to see and hear and therefore you don't get the whole story on that topic. The media can control you by what it produces and as human nature goes, we create an opinion by what we see and hear. This world has seen major chaos just because of a particular news item and people formed their opinion from it. But God says in the Bible in; 2 Corinthians 5:7, *"For we walk by faith and not by sight"* and like other things that God says for us to do is many times opposite of what the world wants us to do.

This is where people have a hard time following or believing in God because he asks us to do things that are opposite of how we have grown up in this world.

Remember the slogan, *"Seeing is believing"* or *"The proof is in the pudding?"* I'm sure there are others but you get the point. The world teaches us to make decisions based upon what we hear and see. What then is *"intuition"* or *"inspiration?"* Where do these thoughts come from?

When police officers investigate a case, they use their intuition to help solve the crime or situation. These are thoughts usually based upon previous experience or some obtained knowledge and training. When a musician writes a song, where does he get his thoughts for songs? Where does he get "inspiration" for music? Where do ANY thoughts come from?

God through his son, Jesus Christ, is establishing a kingdom based upon followers of Jesus receiving revelations from God through reading the Bible. He is not trying to set up a church but a kingdom in which he is Lord and will rule this earth and the universe.

Now what I have just stated sounds like something out of an alien movie but that is a perfect example of how Satan works! If God gives you thoughts and Satan is trying to do the same thing with his thoughts, then what you truly have is a battlefield of the mind! Whatever touches your senses the strongest will dominate your thinking, good or bad. You have heard the saying, *"Garbage in, garbage out".* Jesus said in the Bible, *"For whatever is in your heart, determines what you will say."*

We live in a world that dictates us what is popular, what we should wear, and how we should act with a bottle of beer!

We all tend to become like the people we hang with because of the need to be needed and that is a part of a culture. That's how gangs form. This is why it is so important to attend a church with fellow believers because we have the Gospel in common. You could say that a church fellowship is a form of a gang! Cops hang with cops, firemen hang with firemen. The old saying, *"Birds of a feather, flock together."* It's all the same concept.

So, as the initial question asks, what does God want with you? To keep it simple right here, all humanity since Adam has sinned or to put it another way, we have violated God's laws. God sent his son Jesus here in the flesh to take upon Him the punishment we deserve for those violations. Just like in court, when people get arrested and convicted, a punishment is implemented for the offense committed.

We all have violated *(sinned)* God's laws but because of God's love for us, which is so beyond our ability to understand, Jesus went to the cross and paid in full your violations. What God wants from you is for you to accept that fact and let Jesus run your life which will give you the ability to overcome any circumstance you get involved in. He never said to join a religion!

All the religions of the world are manmade. This doesn't mean that your life now will be a holiday but it means that you now have God giving you wisdom for your life aside from the fact that Jesus Christ is the only way to get to heaven when you die.

Once you decide to accept what Jesus did for you, you will begin a journey that really will change your life as it did mine and millions of others. It won't be easy and there will be times you want to quit, but that is when you hang with others who are strong in their faith. Remember, having faith means believing in something that doesn't meet your eye!

You know that you have rounds in your weapon but guns do jam at times so faith is believing that it will not jam. It's the same with God. When you read the Bible, you take it by faith that what God says is true without you seeing it right now. If you saw it, then there is no faith. What builds your faith is hearing others who have walked their faith in God and came out of their situations.

The bottom line is that God wants you to accept Jesus into your life, ask him to forgive you of your sins *(violations of God's laws)* and go to a Bible believing church in order to fellowship and grow as a Christian. Then as you grow, God wants you to do the same thing I am doing here in this book and that is telling people of what God has done and will do.

> ## **Proverbs 16:9**
> A man's heart plans his way,
> but the Lord determines his steps.

About The Author
Officer Robert D. Faubel, Ret.
"Chaplain Bob"

Investigations into solving crimes involves many things police officers have to consider. One of the main items considered are testimonies of those directly or indirectly involved in a particular incident. These testimonies can validate information about the incident that can lead law enforcement to come to a conclusion and resolve the case. The definition of the word testimony is:

"A formal written or spoken statement, especially one given in a court of law; evidence, sworn statement, attestation, evidence or proof provided by the existence or appearance of something."

In my career as a police officer, I experienced many testimonies from cases that I dealt with as well as cases from other officers. The problem with some testimonies is that the people were not telling the truth which of course can lead an officer into the wrong direction about solving cases. But there were many testimonies that were truthful and valid and in the end of the case verified the original claim of an incident or crime.

This is my first book and it is my testimony of growing up in a family that did not go to church, a father who was an atheist and a mother who was Catholic. As I mentioned above, a testimony is only as good as what it produces in the end. My experiences since 1982 changed my life forever and is the foundation for writing this book. My sole intention is to use this book to tell my testimony and the reader to consider their relationship with God and his Son, Jesus Christ. *This book is really not about me but what God has done in my life.* There are no words that I can express about the peace I have from having a personal relationship with Jesus Christ as my Lord! I was once an atheist but now I'm a Disciple for Jesus Christ!

This is my witness.

Chaplain Bob served as a Special Police Officer and a full time regular Police Officer with the Danbury Police Department, Danbury, CT. He was also a Deputy Sheriff with the Fairfield County Court system.

Bob also is a graphics designer and video editor. He is hired to produce printed materials and creates and edits videos. Contact Bob for information to hire him for your printed needs or video.

Bob has two children, Christen and Aron, from a previous marriage. Bob resides in New Jersey.

Salvation

Synopsis: God created everything. He created 3 main archangels, Gabriel, Michael and Lucifer. Lucifer(Satan) was in charge of music. Lucifer thought that he could do better than God and wanted to take over heaven. Well, so much for strategic planning! God kicked his butt back to Earth and a third of the angels that went along with Satan. Those angels are the demons that are here today on earth working at Satan's requests to destroy this world that God created.

God then created Adam and Eve who as you know screwed up and got kicked out of the Garden of Eden. This was the first *"sin"* and because of that, everyone since then is under sin.

Basically, sin is a crime against God's laws. We all are sinners because of it. Therefore because of the love that God has for us, he made a way that would get us off the hook. It's called ***"SALVATION"***.

This basically means that the human race is doomed to go to hell for eternity unless they accept what God did for us in sending his son, Jesus, down here to earth to take upon Himself the punishment that we deserve for the crimes *(sins)* that we all commit. God gave us the ability to choose and accept what Jesus did for us. God will not force anyone because He loves and gave u free will.

When I first heard this, all I could think of that this was a sci-fi story made up. Yes, there are some movies that actually have this type of scenario but they are only movies. What Jesus did is historical fact.

It comes down to whether or not you believe what I have expressed. Having been an atheist, it was hard for me to accept this but as a cop, I had investigated cases to find the truth. It's the same way with what the Bible claims to be true. It was hard for me to accept that there are demons creating all this turmoil in the world today and Satan hates Christians because of what God did to him.

I have been down the road of trying explain away the origin of mankind using evolution but that didn't work. I came up with some reasonable assumptions without proof of what I was saying. We live in a world of "seeing is believing" as I have stated before in this book. That's how I grew up. But as a cop investigating a crime, you can't just go by what you see.

In 1982 I said a prayer asking God to reveal himself to me and that I would give my life to him to run. I made Jesus Christ my Lord. If you have not done this, I am asking you to seriously consider seeking God and turning your life over to Him. It's a simple task. It's called prayer. God wants your heart. God truly loves you know matter what you have done in the past.

Salvation is just asking God to forgive you of your sins *("crimes")* and asking Jesus to be your Lord and Savior. There are no special words you have to say but say that prayer *from your heart*. God wants you to give your life to Him freely because He can see your hearts' intentions 24/7.

If you have said that prayer, please contact me. I would like to pray with you and help you learn more about what God has for you.

Contact Chaplain Bob

Bob's education to serve others includes having degrees in Psychology, Theology and is an ordained, licensed Chaplain. Bob currently resides in New Jersey.

Chaplain Bob is available on occasion to present his testimony.

chaplain406@gmail.com

chaplainbob@chaplainbob.com

www.chaplainbob.com

www.facebook.com/chaplainfaubel

Chaplain Bob is a member of these organizations

What is a Police Chaplain?

No one is confronted with more situations that demoralize and create emotional, mental and spiritual burdens than today's law enforcement officer. These burdens also affect the officer's family and other members of his or her department. Law enforcement agencies need the specialized guidance, counseling and assistance that Police Chaplains can provide. From the International Conference of Police Chaplains: A law enforcement chaplain is a clergy person with a passionate interest in, and the specialized training for pastoral care in the dangerous world of law enforcement. This pastoral care is offered to all people, regardless of race, gender, sexual orientation, national origin, creed, or religion. It is offered without cost or proselytizing.

The law enforcement chaplain is led in his or her own faith to be available and ready to serve those in need. The chaplain's ministry provides a source of strength to the law enforcement officers and their families, other department members, the community, and the incarcerated. Chaplains listen and participate in the workplace of law enforcement officers with empathy and experience, advising calmly in the midst of turmoil and danger, and offering assistance when appropriate or requested.

What does a Police Chaplain do?

- The duties of the Police Chaplain may include, but are not limited to:
- Riding along with officers on routine patrol on various shifts.
- Accompanying a police officer to assist with notification of any suicide, death or serious injury.
- Working with police officers to assist in any kind of crisis situation where the presence of a chaplain might help.
- Counseling Department members in response to stress or family crisis problems.
- Any such assistance will be privileged and confidential between the officer and chaplain involved.
- Visiting with sick or injured members of the Department at their home or in the hospital.
- Helping organize Department response to ceremonies for officers killed in the line of duty.
- Offering prayers at special occasions such as recruit graduations, award ceremonies and dedications of buildings, etc.
- Advising the Chief of Police in all matters of a religious nature involving the Police Department and performance of law enforcement duties in the community.
- Further, Chaplains shall act as liaison with local ministerial associations and on matters pertaining to

the moral, spiritual, and religious welfare of police personnel. Assisting the Police Department in the performance of appropriate ceremonial functions.

- Assisting in the provision of planned, scheduled training to police personnel. Training may include orientation as a new employee, Academy training, roll call training, spouse orientation, etc.
- Providing practical assistance to victims. Assisting at suicide incidents.

Church Security

In today's world, safety and security are becoming a growing concern within churches and various houses of worship. This was never even a thought years ago but with the violence increasing in today's society and the attacks on churches increasing, the establishment of some sort of security teams in churches is becoming a necessity. Churches can be held liable for not having some sort of security team!

Sadly, the only thing many church members, staff and volunteers think about when the concept of church safety and security is mentioned, is responding to a shooter or to an assault on the church on Sunday or Wednesday or whenever your services are held. There is so much more to having a truly safe and secure church than that---as important as that is, of course.

This statement is expressed in so many situations:

"We didn't think it would happen here!"

Chaplain Bob is a church security consultant. Contact him if you have any questions.

Bob on TBN's, "Praise The Lord" TV show

Bob worked for various security companies

Bob and Chaplain Santos   Bob doing "ride-along" as chaplain

Scriptures Passages to Remember

John 3:16: *"For God loved the world in this way:[a] He gave His One and Only Son, so that everyone who believes in Him will not perish but have eternal life.*

Proverbs 18:21: *Life and death are in the power of the tongue, and those who love it will eat its fruit.".*

John 3:3: *"Jesus replied, "I assure you: Unless someone is born again, he cannot see the kingdom of God."*

2 Corinthians 4:4: *In their case, the god of this age has blinded the minds of the unbelievers so they cannot see the light of the gospel of the glory of Christ, who is the image of God.*

Acts 2:21: *Then everyone who calls on the name of the Lord will be saved.*

Proverbs 3:5-6: *Trust in the Lord with all your heart and lean not to your understanding but in all your ways, seek Him and He will direct your steps.*

Romans 13
Submitting to the Government
(Police Officer in the Bible)

1. Everyone must submit to the governing authorities, for there is no authority except from God, and those that exist are instituted by God. 2. So then, the one who resists the authority is opposing God's command, and those who oppose it will bring judgment on themselves. 3. For rulers are not a terror to good conduct, but to bad. Do you want to be unafraid of the authority? Do what is good, and you will have its approval. 4. For government is *God's servant* for your good. But if you do wrong, be afraid, because it does not carry the sword for no reason. For government is *God's servant*, an avenger that brings wrath on the one who does wrong. 5. Therefore, you must submit, not only because of wrath, but also because of your conscience. 6. And for this reason you pay taxes, since the authorities are *God's public servants*, continually attending to these tasks. 7. Pay your obligations to everyone: taxes to those you owe taxes, tolls to those you owe tolls, respect to those you owe respect, and honor to those you owe honor.

THE ARMS OF A COP

By Officer Bob Faubel, Ret.
Police Chaplain

Whose arms separate the husband and wife in a
domestic?
Whose arms delivers babies in the back of a cruiser?
Whose arms stop traffic to cross old ladies?
Whose arms carry a dead child from a car?
Whose arms comfort the mother?
The arms of a cop.

Who gets spit at by kids?
Who has to work a second job to afford to live?
Who has to wear a bullet proof vest?
Who has the authority to shoot a fellow human being?
Who has to live with the responsibility of when to
shoot? **A cop.**

Who walks a beat in the snow and rain at 3 am?
Who risks his life every time he puts on the uniform?
Who pursues cars at 100 mph in traffic?
Who works all types of shifts and holidays?
Who looks for your runaway kid?
A cop.

Whose arms fight crooks, sees death, get stressed
out, and goes home to a family with a smile?

Whose arms have to restrain a mother when she finds her son dead from drug overdose?
Whose arms issue a parking ticket only for the driver to stab him for doing his job?
Whose arms wrestle crooks with aids then goes home to hug his spouse and children?
The arms of a cop.

Who has to have all the answers but is always wrong in the eyes of the public?
Who has to be a lawyer, doctor, counselor, fireman, plumber, auto mechanic, family therapist, and child psychologist? Whose arms have to be faster than a speeding bullet, more powerful than a locomotive, and able to leap tall buildings at a single bound?
The arms of a cop.

Whose arms minister to people and whose job was created and ordained by God?
Whose arms may never know the power to overcome stress
or the ability to obtain strength from God and who may die in sin
because he was never told the truth about Jesus Christ.

The arms of a cop.

Endogenements

In a world filled with so much chaos and confusion it's refreshing to hear the victorious journey of my brother and friend Officer Bob Faubel. In his book "Put Your Hands Up" Bob captures and releases that joy that comes from knowing the giver of life in a simple easy to read testimony that many will identify with.

I first met Bob many years ago sharing my testimony at a local Christian organization, Bob was a true delight. I was a former heroin addict from the music business that God had transformed into a servant for His kingdom. Bob had been on the flip side of life serving as a Police Officer. "But God" who transformed us both and called us into His service as Law Enforcement Chaplains to help the everyday hurting hero's that serve us all so well. So sit back put your hands up and enjoy the read.

Walter J Santos

Chaplain
United States Secret Service
www.santosministries.org
email waltersantos@mac.com
mobile 619-993-1133

Endorsements

"There is nothing better than a personal testimony of how God draws each of us to Himself. Chaplain, and retired Police Officer, Bob Faubel gave his book the perfect title, "Put Your Hands Up! (An Arrest Warrant from God)" Not only was there no silver spoon in Bob's mouth growing up as an only child, there was no mention of God either but that did not stop God. From childhood, school, college, navy and finally a police officer Bob shares how, even with no interest in God personally, God had interest in him. One of my favorite parts was when Bob saw "Hands Up" in an entirely different light than he was use to as a cop! I encourage you to walk with Bob through his journey and as you do think about your own journey and where you are right now.

Paul Lee

(Retired Captain, Chattanooga P.D.)
Executive Director
Fellowship of Christian Peace Officers–USA
www.fcpo.org

Endorsements

I could really relate to Bob and his story of finding God as a police officer. His honesty and transparency is very compelling , I believe people can relate and connect to his story. Especially Police officer's who have a lot of issues I need to hear it's OK to find God! I suggest this book for all active and retired law-enforcement. Also for anyone who wants to hear a good story of a life turned around because of a personal relationship with Jesus Christ.

Pastor Andrew Columbia
Former NYPD Officer

Billy Graham Rapid Response Team Chaplain, and Speaker.
Author of "Transformed".

MCB Church
76 Gleneida Ave.
Carmel, NY 10512
www.mcbchurch.org
www.mtcarmelbaptistchu.wixsite.com

Endorsements

"It is a privilege to endorse more than a book, but an icon of faithfulness in Christian ministry. Bob and his story represent the undeniable power of God to change a human life."

Pastor Carlos Aviles, Jr.

Retired Detective NYPD

Calvary Chapel
115 Bloxam Avenue
Clermont, FL 34711
352-708-6083
www.cclermont.org/
ccclermontfl@gmail.com

Endorsements

I have known Bob for many years through Law Enforcement and then through church. Bob is one of the finest men I have ever met and one of god greatest warriors today. In reading Bob's book I was reminded of many things in my upbringing that I had put in a closet in the back of my mind.

The abused of my alcoholic father how I watched him beat my mom in his drunken rage and then me as a kid. The switch, wooden spoons, belt and as I got older his fist up till I was 18. It reminded me of my alcoholism and I had a 25 year anniversary of sobriety coming up on May 30.

I have not talked much about my alcoholism as I was ashamed of it for years. But with such a big anniversary coming up and after reading Bob's book I was inspired to speak about it and go public to all my friends, family,facebook friends and 37 thousand active and retired police officer.

Reading Bob's book was not by chance cause I don't read books but it was god's plan that I read it and he used Bob as a messenger to me. I am not so ashamed any more and I am proud of my 25 years of sobriety.

My message to others was god doing it through Bob and his book god told me to tell my story, well that was only part of it but the rest is for another day. Thank you Bob for being a friend and helping me to overcome a big obstacle in my life and thank you God for using Bob.

Raymond Pacheco

Retired Police Officer
Bethel, Police Department
Bethel Connecticut

rrprotective@gmail.com

Resources

Fellowship of Christian Peace Officers-USA

2158 Northgate Park Lane,

Suite 413

Chattanooga, TN 37415

Phone: 423-553-8806   Email: fcpo@fcpo.org

Officer Down Memorial Page

PO Box 1047

Fairfax, Virginia, 22038-1047

National Law Enforcement Officers Memorial Fund

901 E Street, NW | Suite 100

Washington, DC 20004-2025

202.737.3400 fax 202.737.3405 info@nleomf.org

COPLINE
Law Enforcement Officers' Hotline
AN OFFICER'S LIFELINE
COPLINE: 1-800-COPLINE
1-800-267-5463

Concerns of Police Survivors

Mail: P.O. Box 3199 - Camdenton, MO 65020

Physical: 846 Old South 5 - Camdenton, MO 65020

Phone: 573-346-4911

Fax: 573-346-1414

Email: cops@nationalcops.org

Resources

International Conference of Police Chaplains

PO Box 5590

Destin, FL   32540

t. 850.654.9736

f. 850.654.9742

ICPC@icpc4cops.org

Suicide Prevention Resource Center

Education Development Center, Inc.

1025 Thomas Jefferson Street, NW, Suite 700

Washington, DC 20007

Police Officers For Christ NYPD

P.O. Box 1044- Peck Slip Station

New York, NY 10272

(929)-285-9682

pofcnypd@pofcnypd.org

Santos Ministries

PO Box 1415

Hightstown, NJ 08520

Phone: (619) 993-1133

santosministries.org

Resources

All items custom designed by Chaplain Bob

Additional Books Available through

PoBoy Publishing:

"Works Revisited" (Amazon/KDP)

"Mormonism Revisited"
(Amazon/KDP)

"The Watchtower Revisited, Dangerous
Doctrines of Jehovah's Witnesses"
(Amazon/KDP)

"The Importance of Just One Revisited"
(Amazon/KDP)

For quantity discounts please write:
PoBoy Publishing
125 Hidden Hills Dr.
Ormond Beach, Fl. 32174
Email: rev.stuw@yahoo.com

© 2019

Made in the USA
Middletown, DE
03 November 2023

41857914R00083